So Pretty . . . . So Many Tears

Minu

authorHOUSE®

AuthorHouse™
1663 Liberty Drive
Bloomington, IN 47403
www.authorhouse.com
Phone: 1-800-839-8640

Published by AuthorHouse   04/04/2012

ISBN: 978-1-4567-4587-5 (sc)
ISBN: 978-1-4685-6642-0 (e)

*Any people depicted in stock imagery provided by Thinkstock are models,
and such images are being used for illustrative purposes only.
Certain stock imagery © Thinkstock.*

This book is printed on acid-free paper.

Contents

DEDICATION

This book is dedicated to "The Love Of My Life" who loved me in such a way that I had never been loved before. He was beautiful to me, he truly loved me unconditionally. For I was once told, "When someone doesn't love you, everything you do is wrong but when someone loves you, nothing you do is wrong!"

"The Love of My Life," was everything to me, his name was Tony Cota. He died when he was 27 years old. He loved me so much, he never had to ever tell me, I could feel it! When you find "True love," or "Real love," always remember that it will not be a question for you to ask, whether he or she loves you or not, it will be apparent! You will not have to ask them if they love you, you will feel it so strong that you will tell everyone that he/she loves you! You will want to tell everyone in the world and shout it from the top of the highest mountain! When you feel like that, then you know you have found True Love! So many, many people to this day, wish and hope to find that kind of love, they have never ever felt what it is to be loved this way or have love this way, "True Love."

Well, I am so blessed that I have found love this way and although, he left this world and everyday, I still cry so hard even though it's already been 25 years, I still cry because I miss the other half of me! He was so much apart of me, whether he told me or not, I cannot and still do not want to live without him! Still after all these years, I find it so damn hard when I wake up and I do not see his face. Life for me is so hard still that I couldn't go with him too! I wish that someone would go find him for me! Please! This is how much I love him! Still! I know that if it had been me that left this world, he would be missing me this much too! I just know it to be true!

All I have to say, because if it is about him I could go on and on about "Our Love," but I do have to say that if you ever find True Love like this one, keep it! Do not let go of it! Never let it go from your sight! Do not let anyone get it the middle of it and take it from you because once you find it, there are and will be so many jealous people over your love and will definitely try to hurt it for they will always be jealous of Love that anyone has that is real, because they do not have it.

The poems from the book were written from my heart and there are some poems that were written by my granddaughter Vanessa Rose, along with some poems that were written by my daughters, Desiree Grace and Princess Anna. The poems that were written by them were wonderful to me and I thank them for being so loving and true.

The poems that were written by me, some were written when I was 16 years of age, and from that day on, until the days of what is called "The Present Day." They are poems from all different types of feelings and there are also different type of styles of poems written, not just one type or style.

INTRODUCTION

LOVE IS

The strongest emotion in the World is Love. It's strength lies in how it makes one feel and what it can cause one to do. People will die for it—people will kill for it- and most of all—Jesus died for it, was crucified for it, tortured because of it, spit on for it, and hated for it! This kind of Love is Real love, Pure Love, True Love, Unconditional Love, this kind of love comes from God.

GOD'S LOVE—

It takes a lot of a certain kind of love to be able to love someone still after they have deliberately hurt you, spit on you, hit and beat you, hate you, having taken advantage of you and simply by their actions showing that they just do not love you over and over again! Not very many people can still love someone after all of that, let alone even forgive someone for causing so much hurt to them. To forgive someone for that kind of pain caused on you and to still love them is purely straight from GOD - and simply put GOD IS LOVE! To endure this kind of pain in your heart and soul and to still have it in your heart and ability to still love anyone at all that is so hurtful and hateful is such a completely unselfish act and means that you must be full of God's sort of love. If you have ever had this sort of love then you must realize that God has blessed you with this ability to love this way. For anyone to have this kind of love and to love someone like that is absolutely spiritual, sacred, and a blessing to be in that level in your life because it is very difficult to reach that level in one's life. For instance; to forgive someone, to be able to forgive anyone that has put you through great hurt, severe pain and such evil torment is very difficult instead of wanting to hurt back and get revenge. It is not very easy for anyone to forgive without trying to hurt back but Jesus did it and God keeps doing it for us.

To Forgive: To Forgive is DIVINE. I have always taught my children to forgive, to have a forgiving heart, to not carry hatred and bitterness in their heart, to give their hurt and anger to God and to let God deal with our pain and suffering and as hard as it was for them, as I have seen my children in their lives now, I can see the growth and maturity in their hearts, I have witnessed their loving hearts with the kind of love that only God can give and have for I know that they all have learned to forgive! It takes someone very special to be able to forgive and really never hold a grudge for hurt being caused against them. God forgives us each and every day—every minute—every second—once we declare that we are sorry for our unforgivable actions, for the hurt that we have caused on others and ourselves, even though maybe we may not have even realized that we have hurt someone else in our lives, but all it takes is for us to just ask him to forgive and there it is, we are forgiven.

I believe sincerely, that all of us, all of you in the theory, thought, principle and/or the reality of that **<u>people know not what they do</u>**—this is so true about everyone of us! I have realized this even in my own life and I also realize that if I had known what I was actually doing to someone when I have hurt them I know truly that I would not have hurt anyone. Had I really known the result of the hurt and the consequences of my hurting them, I would never had done anything to hurt them! For so often in our lives when we hurt someone so much, the consequences are that we hurt ourselves; therefore if more of us knew what we were really doing to one another, and the consequences of our hurt that we cause even to others really brings, I like to believe that more of us would not cause hurt. This is also what Jesus proclaimed when he asked God to forgive the bad people for what they had done to him; Jesus said, "They know not what they do." Most people don't realize the severe consequences of what actions they take, even so, more so, they do not realize that they can be causing severe damage and changes to even themselves, forever! If we try to remember this about the people that cause us pain and people that we hurt then it might help us to understand that we are all too are ignorant to the fact of what hurt causes for all of us and others and what has really been done and what their hurt did or can do.

Once they become wise to what has been done, again, I truly believe that most of everyone would be sorry for what they have done and/or would really not cause the hurt at all. When you hurt someone so deeply and wrongly, you hurt yourself whether you believe it or not, you will carry guilt with what you do, or with what you did, whether you realize it or not. Guilt will destroy your soul, for guilt can actually kill, it will eat you up inside, it will bring hurt to you and even cause you not want to live anymore, with yourself or with what you have done. Eventually, it will get to you, somehow, someway in your life.

Not very many people have Pure love; Pure love is forgiving someone of hurting you and even killing your spirit—your joy—your good heart, your pure goodness or even trying to kill all of our love inside, especially those that have caused us such great harm and we feel they are responsible for the loss in our lives.

This kind of Pure Love only comes from God—Himself. When you have this kind of love—you know that someone who has done you wrong doesn't <u>deserve</u> to be forgiven, and in reality none of us who wrong someone <u>deserve</u> to be forgiven at all! By God Himself and the kind of love that comes from God Himself, who forgives without even trying to; when we have Pure Love inside of us and it is in our hearts naturally, when we forgive such as this way, it is not necessarily because we are weak or afraid of anyone, it is only because we do have that kind of love in our hearts; the kind of love that God is purely about. One cannot help himself, one cannot help but forgive for it is in their nature because it is of God's nature to be Love and only Love.

Some of us believe that when we wrong someone we advance our chances of eternal damnation, you would think that this should give us some kind of remorse knowing we will still be dealt with and that we might be in danger of losing our very own souls! Therefore, it is also believed that we should have mercy and compassion on people who have wronged us, leaving revenge to whom it really belongs to . . . God. Compassion is what God is about. Compassion comes from True Love, Pure Love, and when you have Compassion, you have what God is about and that this exists inside of your own hearts and thus, you have Mercy. With the Grace of God, is one able to even have the compassion and mercy enough in their hearts to forgive, because as I have written, To Forgive Is Divine. It is so true when they say that only Love can heal a broken heart and yet, love can cause a broken heart. There is so much irony in this life of ours but the key to being happy is learning all about Pure Love, True Love, God's Love and once we have those we have Compassion and Mercy.

Forgiving someone for what they have done to you also helps the wrong person learn what Love is, for anyone who has wronged and hurt someone is obviously lacking Real Love, and therefore needs to learn what they have really done! Most people in this world do not know what Real Love is unless they have truly felt it in their hearts and until they have truly felt what Real Love is, how can they learn what they need to learn when they hurt someone. Not knowing Real Love keeps them in ignorance of what they have done and can actually keep them hurting inside of their own souls and this also keeps them in the cycle that they are stuck in, so helping them learn and feel Real Love, releases their bond from being stuck in the endless cycle of hurting themselves as well as sinning against others. For as long as they are sinning and hurting others, they do not realize that they are really hurting themselves and whether they know this or not, they are condemning themselves, they really do not need us to condemn them any further! Knowing that they may be damned forever and having wisdom that only comes from God, will allow you to realize that by forgiving someone who has hurt you will also help them not only get closer to knowing Real Love, but allows you to stay in God's Realm of Love and Mercy, leading you to living forever with the Pure Love that Lord God gives us. Knowing that you have helped someone get closer to this kind of Love also brings you to the Pure Love of the Universe which most of the people know as God and His Love and doing what our souls are supposed to do, what we were put here on earth to do is simply love eachother. By not forgiving those that have hurt us, we keep ourselves also stuck in a bitter cycle of hatred with bitterness and hurt inside of our own souls and therefore we are preventing ourselves from climbing to the stairway of Heaven or advancing to the next level of our lifetimes, which is where we truly belong. So when we forgive those that hurt us, not only are we releasing those that hurt us but we are releasing ourselves from the bitterness and ugliness that comes from holding on to hatred and bitterness that keeps our souls trapped which keeps us from being Godly and keeps us in the cycle of hurt and also keeps us from growth.

When we do not forgive others, or ourselves or allow others to forgive us for whatever it is or was that we did. It will keep us stuck, stuck in box that if we do not learn about forgiveness, we will never get out of that box. We will stay stagnant in a negative cycle and eventually in a negative world. By showing others, Pure Love, Real Love, and True Love it makes you a better person which evil does not want you to be, for evilness, in whatever form continues to exist and to keep you in that bad cycle and all it does is cause you to hurt back, keeping hurt inside and secretly you are wishing those that hurt you to be hurt back, and thus keeping yourself full of hate and hurt which is not from God. Once we release all of our hurts and pain, inside of our hearts we feel so much better and happier, it is so wonderful to feel this feeling, it is a miracle that forgiving someone can also make us happier people and happier in life!

Holding on to the hurt and pain is not what we should do in our lives for if we hold on to hurt and pain from others trying to punish them without allowing life itself to do what it is supposed to do (which is allowing them to get what they deserved all by themselves) keeps us from being forgiven for any wrong that we may have done onto others in our life. This holds you captive in your own wrong doing and in your own guilt of anything you may have done in your life to others and to yourself. Therefore, when you hold on to hurt, hate and bad feelings, you hold yourself down, keeping your spirit at a negative level only drawing negative things and negative people to you, which thus draws nothing but negative actions back to you.

The most important way to show others Real Love, God's Love, is to just purely Love them, which comes with Forgiveness for what they have done to you, and even forgiving ourselves for what we have done to ourselves or have not done! It is not our job to judge and condemn. Condemning ourselves can cause so much damage to our lives and to the growth of our lives, that sometimes that damage can become irreparable. That job (condemning or judging) is for Life itself, of course, God and if you hold on to hurt, hate, envy, jealousy, and bitterness you are trying to do what you are not supposed to do, you are trying to do God's job! Trying to get revenge on someone is only going to cause more negative to be brought down upon yourself and those closest to you. With the most wisest kind of love in your heart, all you need to do is love yourself and others and you do not have to try to take revenge upon anyone.

Letting go of any hurt or pain even if it is for your happiness, it gives you strength within yourself and when there is that kind of love and strength within you, you will have "Pure Love." The strength of this kind of Love can conquer any hatred or any negative feelings that might cause any more pain, when nothing else can conquer it. When you have this kind of love, you are blessed in so many ways, more blessed than the richest man or woman in the world! You have something that no one person can buy. Real Love, True Love, Undying Love, and Unconditional Love, is something that no money in the whole world. This kind of love is priceless and it's road is the only road that leads to the "Gateway to Heaven," the Gateway to True Happiness that nothing else but love and wisdom has. You do not have to do anything to those that have hurt you when you have wisdom and love. You bring Power into yourself and your realm that you are living in when you have this kind of love. Having wisdom and love, you have Power in your mind, body and soul so much that it causes a kind of energy (good energy) that your body can even heal or even cause you to look and feel younger than when you are filled with ugliness and meanness, which can cause one to look old and ugly. Even when I was a very young girl, I would always try to thank the Lord for each brand new day that he gave me, there were times I would forget to thank him and I would always feel so bad. I would feel as if I was a bad girl but as I grew I begin to acknowledge the difference between bad and good and I also learned that there is so much gray in the world. Not every thing that we go through, not every person that we meet, not all that we see or hear is definitely completely solid or even as they may seem to be. All we can do is try each day to make it a beautiful day for ourselves and the people that we love, whether it is a good day or not. I grew to know that each day is a beautiful day if we make it a good day and it all depends on our attitudes about what has happened in our life. It should be a beautiful day just because we are still here while we are still here in our lives, we are all still a part of this world and whether we believe it or not, we are all a part of each other and what affects one, truly affects us all!

My father always tried to remind me when something bad would happen to me that something good would always come from it, so he wanted me to keep in mind that even the bad days would be good days. So now I thank God for even the bad days, because even the bad days taught me how to be a better person just by teaching me patience, discipline, and most of all Love! So this is what I remind myself always and I always try to thank God for even the struggles in my life and there have been so many difficult times that I have had to endure but I also know that there a lot more people in this world that have it worse or have had it worse. When I think of all of the people that have been through worse than I have, even though I have been through a lot, it helps me focus on just how blessed I am and how blessed I have been and how much Love God has for me and how protected by him I really am. For those people that do not believe in God, they can call it Karma, or fate but either way you try to see it, Love really comes and goes around. If you give it, you will receive it, you get what you give in this lifetime and in every lifetime after. For I do believe in other lifetimes, I refuse to believe that God just gave us one, I believe he gave us more than one to help us become better human beings and in order to become better, we need more than one lifetime to change or make changes and learn through all of our mistakes, I believe this with all my heart. This only tells me that this is how much Love God really has for all of us in this world and if God is just a Great Bigger Entity than all of us but that this Entity is in charge somehow, than this entity knows what and how to do things including how to cause Love to be a better thing in this world and this shows me that no matter what, Love is what it is all about. God is said to be Love, so therefore, God being Love, there it is!

I have 12 children and 17 grandchildren. Having 12 children are not part of the difficult times and struggles, although it is very hard bringing up so many children and trying to make them all become beautiful and good people and for them to know the difference. Too much and too little of giving and taking and knowing and remembering to hug my children even when times are so bad with all that happens in life that try to come in your life and make your life bad and in the middle of all that, still trying to remember to tell your children that they are important and that you love them and that they matter because nothing is their fault and yes, I wanted this many children! I chose to have that many children, I wanted a lot of children, because I always felt so alone, being the only daughter with five brothers, that I thought if I had many children, I would always feel loved! For whatever reason, I chose to have my children, I knew that because it was I that chose to have them, that it was I and only I that needed to make sure that I brought them up with love and goodness in their hearts! The struggles began when I had all my children, I did it basically alone! I didn't know or think that I was going to be basically alone with a father not around, but when it happened, I hoped and prayed that God became their father and that, that is what they needed in their life!

Believe it or not, because of the types of two husbands that I had and because I was blessed with learning the hard way of trying not to change my life and destiny, I basically had to bring up my children alone but then again, that is a different story in itself that needs to be told. But I still thank God each day for blessing me with 12 children! Believe me, with all of my children, there have been more than just struggles in my life but thank God, my children he has blessed me with are all beautiful as well as all my 17 grandchildren. When I write "Beautiful" I mean beautiful in their hearts for I taught them all one good quality to learn and to have and that is to have

Forgiveness! Besides all the other main stuff that I taught my children, like manners, good etiquette, good language, to be strong and independent and not to be stubborn in life, to love and to be loved and to know the difference of many, many emotions and feelings and what to expect in life and what not to expect in life and most of all, that no one, NO ONE, even myself, is perfect but to have love anyway! To have love for life itself and and for everyone that comes in their world and to remember to try to laugh a lot and let things go!

I still try to thank God for each day, every morning, that I am alive and that I am still alive in this world for my children and family that I feel need me. Not all the times I remember in the morning, sometimes, I remember at night and whatever time it is, I thank God for what he has blessed me with, even when times have been "not so good." All I know is that each day that I live, so far, I know that the Lord needs and deserves my praise and I pray to Him every chance I get, even in the middle of conversations, in the middle of movies, in the middle of yelling and fighting. I always pray to him in the beginning and with the most important prayer that I have come to know as <u>His Prayer;</u> is always said even with all my children! So I dedicate this book to The Lord and I will pray now as I do whenever I do anything, as I ask him to continue to bless me because even with the times of my homelessness, abandonments, abuses, bringing my children up alone and now with my illnesses that I have and still endure. I always thank Him for I know that even with all of the bad I have gone through, I have become a better person and learned from all of what I have gone through, thanks to God.

Our Father

OUR FATHER WHO ART IN HEAVEN
HALLOWED BE THY NAME
THY KINGDOM COME THY WILL BE DONE
ON EARTH AS IT IS IN HEAVEN
GIVE US THIS DAY OUR DAILY BREAD
AND FORGIVE US OUR TRESPASSES
AS WE FORGIVE THOSE WHO TRESPASS AGAINST US
AND LEAD US NOT INTO TEMPTATION
BUT DELIVER US FROM EVIL

FOR THINE IS THE KINGDOM, THE POWER
AND GLORY FOREVER AND EVER

AMEN

Hell Here

JUST LIVING IN HELL HERE EVERY SINGLE DAY
WITH THE PASSING HOURS OF ONGOING PAIN

THE SIGHS THE MOANS OF MY HURT GO ON
ANGER TIRED EARS HEARING MY PAIN SONG

COMPREHENDING SECONDS OF RELIEF PRAYED FOR?
SLEEP IS MY HEAVEN IN HELL HERE I LIVE AMONG

PAIN HURTING SO BAD YET I TRY TO MANAGE A SMILE
THE LOVE OF MY CHILDREN WHY GOD HAS MY STAY

GOD KNEW I WOULD NEED THEM ALONG THIS WAY
THE URGE TO LEAVE MY WORLD TORMENTS ALL THE WHILE

I ASK WHY THIS PAIN IS WHAT I MUST ENDURE
A SIN I COMMITED IN A PAST LIFE IT MUST BE FOR SURE

THE LESSONS I HAVE LEARNED ARE THE WAY IT MUST BE
PAIN UNTIL MY DEATH FROM THIS HELL BRINGING RELIEF

ONLY THEN WILL I FINALLY FIND THE DOOR TO HEAVEN
MY LIFE WILL RETIRE IN PEACE GOD WILL FINALLY GIVE ME

ROSE PORTILLO

Was It You

I WOULD SIT AND WONDER WHO IT WAS SAYING MY NAME
WHO'S VOICE IT WAS I WOULD HEAR CALLING OUT TO ME

ALL THOSE TIMES I WOULD JUST WALK BY NOW A MEMORY
EVEN THEN IT WAS YOU AS I SHED ALL THESE TEARS HERE

ODD I COULD NOT REMEMBER CLEAR THE WAY I DO NOW
NOW I KNOW IT WAS YOU THAT SPOKE TO ME OUTLOUD

YOU WATCHED ME YOU STARED CALLING OUT MY NAME
IT WAS YOU THE ONE TALKING TO ME UNDER THAT TREE

MEMORIES OF YOU WERE VAGUE AND UNKNOWN UNTIL
YOU CAME TO ME WAS IT YOU THAT CALLED OUT MY WILL

I FORGOT THAT IT WAS ONLY YOUR HEAD THAT TURNED
UNTIL PRESENTLY DID THE MEMORY OF YOUR LOVE APPEAR

ALL ALONG DURING ALL THOSE TIMES OF ME BEING BLUE
WALKING ALONE FEELING TERRIBLE NOW I KNOW IT WAS YOU

TELL ME HOW DID YOU KNOW THIS EVEN WAY BACK WHEN
I WOULD HAVE SAID YES IF ONE MORE TIME YOU CALLED AGAIN

AS I TURNED AWAY FROM YOUR VOICE YES IT FELT STRANGE
FOR WAS IT YOU WHO LOVED ME SINCE A VERY YOUNG AGE

ROSE PORTILLO

This Strange Feeling

This Strange Feeling Knowing You From Somewhere Before
Brings Memories Of Being Thrilled With Sweet Love Of Yours
Remembrance Of Our Souls Being Connected In An Ancient Lore
Visioning Our Lives Together Causing Our Souls To Forever Soar

Feeling Those Kisses From Somewhere Ever Since The Age Of Time
Eons Ago Of Moments Ever Since As Our Worlds Had Been Entwined
Twas So Long Since Then But I Always Knew You Would Be Mine
Many Lifetimes Have Passed Between Us Yet Our Love Stays Alive

Yes My Soul Forever Is Meant To Come Back Wearing Your Crown
My Heart Will Always Belong To You So Much As You Know Was True
You Inside My Soul Still Connected All The While Our Spirits Have Flown
The Truth Was Finally Told With Your Blood For I Was Made From You

Our Kisses Had Proven To Be So Familiar From All Those Days Of Old
Unforgotten Brilliantly Enlightened As From The Folds Of A Golden Rose
Strange Though Our Love So Deep Even Within As All The Angels Know
This Strange Feeling Unique That Forever Enriches Inside Our Very Souls

Every Memory Of Our Sweet Love So Bitterly Lost Leaves Me Lonely Still
How Can This Destiny Of Ours Not Exist As This Moment Is All For Reals
Keeping Spirits Close Inside Of Us Timelessly Waiting For Our Love's Mime
Both Of Us Knowing The Intricate Same Heartbeat Deeply Feeling It In Rhyme

Who Were You Really Growing With Me In Those Great Days Of Old My Love?
You Knew Me Before Yet Not Ever Seeing My Eyes Only Til With Me You
Sought
Well Then Who Was I But For Your Love With You Trying To Bring Me Forth
Bringing Pain Without You Waiting Throughout Eternity In This Wretched
Earth

Rose Portillo

My Mothers Creed

When you were all so very little perfect I was not this is true
But you were the only things that mattered to me in this life
The only purpose that was in my life was to live for only you
And that for all of you to be who you are and to be happy

I never stopped to think even once you'd have hate for me
That you'd be bitter or do anything bad towards your mom
I had faith never believing in my heart that any wrong you'd be
Or thinking worse of me I just thought you knew I had to be strong

When you got older you became the you that all of you chose to be
When you began to lie and have hate talking behind my back
My disappointment I tried to hide behind my Love for you
Already knowing that you were trying be what you felt I lacked

It's okay that now you feel that only you know what is best
That I your mother would only just love you with all my heart
I could never be what you expected I should or behave any less
I realize you have never really felt what I will never lose a part

I'm sorry I am not what you wanted or felt that I should be
All I know is I wiped your noses made your food cleaned your home
I never showed you a bad life I worried at nights until you were in bed
It was always ONLY YOU on my mind nothing else only you alone

I left "My Heart's Love" along the way to live my life in sadness for you
It doesn't matter if I love your father more or less for YOU are my heart
Now when it all comes back to me I see what I left is everything I am
You don't even like me blaming me it's always going to be on my part

It was you who chose to stay away I cried hard for you not to leave
I was alone without much help I did my best to give you a good life
I lived only for you to be the best that you could be until you were grown
It was hard being abused being left alone living with a man full of strife

I apologize for all that madness shown that shouldn't have been
Please forgive me for not having all the money that could buy at the time
I didn't want to have to do it alone I wished there was only one dad
I was the only one that strived at least I didn't give up I never lied

I'm hurt by your eagerness to leave I love all of you with all of my heart
I was always home with you I can only ask forgiveness so many times
For I will not keep trying to be in your life if you choose to stay away
It is your way of telling me you do not approve of my life as if it is a crime

When I am gone I want you to know I never wanted it to be this way
I love my mother and father no matter what they were or what they did
I never lost my respect for them for you too will feel the pain some day
It was not their fault they're only human I know their love was real instead

I am only your mother I've done the best I could under the circumstances

Rose Portillo

That Very Moment

It was that very moment of time changed "My Forever"
All the love inside of my heart could never be wrong
Became such a part of Our Essence entering via our hearts
All that had been for us "Our Love" with memories not gone

I knew what you felt that very moment your lips touched mine
The tingling of our spines "Our Love's" energy seemed to be caught
They took your soul but it was all I had left inside of My Being
Ours spirits entangled with the eminence of Our Souls had brought

The day "That Very Moment" our two spirits soared exchanging love
It wasn't our hearts expressing love becoming not part of but One
It was something deeper than anyone had ever felt or ever been told
Our spirits were in the "Depths of Heaven's Realm" through our songs

Not wanting to leave you with only dark sadness still way deep inside
Lifting of love in our spirits to inner depths becoming one in essence of
It was your spirit entwined awesomely taking away my melancholy blues
"That Very Moment" you entered my soul what we both felt only we both know

Rose Portillo

This Pain

This Pain Has Been Laying Hidden For So Very Long
Unknown Unseen By The World I Live In And I Belong

Secretly Forever Seeping Still So Deep Down Into My Bones
Quietly So Convincingly Ever Growing Very Old And Cold

The Pain That Entered Settled In It's New Found Home
Deadlier Than Ever With It's Vile Spreading All On Its Own

Yesterday Stagnant Today With More Growth Until It Is Full
Living Here All The Way Down Inside All The Way Through

A Tale Of Woes When It Has Reached My Veins Alone
For The Death Of My Life Is What Is Planned And Condoned

Rose

Remember Me?

When I First Saw You With This I Knew I Could Love You
Even More Love Carried Within As My Tears Came In Floods
It Was Your Secret Though You Intended Simply To Hide
The Tears Were Hidden All Those Years Yes But I Did Cry

The Truth Was Told But I Think You And I Already Knew
That You Would Leave And You Could Never Be True
You Had No Love For Me It Was All Just Lies Locked Inside
Now You Want Me? Say You Want To Look In My Eyes?

What Do You Want From Me In Your Now Lonely Time?
Do You Really Love Me A Little Or Is This Just Your Crime?
I Believed You Though You Didn't Have To Say You Will
Your Love For Me Now Tell Me Is It All Even For Real?

Rose

Your Spirit Cries

I hear you call when Your Spirit Cries
Crying out in the darkest deepest of nights
All the while crying still with all thy might
I went to you though without fear without fright

I went to where I could still hear your voice roam
Where our spirits had once entwined in a battle storm
So deep our love was within the depths of our inner souls
Where the essence of our spirits left there forever more

Remembering that I turned away but only for a moment!
To return and I couldn't find you! Where did you roam?
Only to feel the pain that had been felt in all our love's hearts
Where their tears still swell and are known alone torn apart

I can still hear you call me from where Your Spirit Cries!
It goes into the deep midst where the tragic blue moon lies
I go now to where I hear only too loud even are your sighs
As I pray to see you there! Searching deep inside my eyes!

Rose Portillo

Your Soft Brown Eyes

As I Remember Moments With You
As My Memory Continues To Linger On,
I Recall Your Beautiful Soft Brown Eyes
It's All In The Story That Was Never Told

As I Walked Into Your Life That One Day
You Said It Was Me You Adored That Way,
You Told Me You Would Live Only For Me
To Spend A Lifetime Together Forever We'd Be

Yes I Remember Your Beautiful Soft Brown Eyes
The Memories Still Painfully Lingers They Don't Lie,
They Haunt My Nights With Deep Sadness Until I Cry
They Hold Secrets That Were Untold Of Lonely Lives

As I Looked Inside Your Beautiful Soft Brown Eyes
The Secrets That Would Unfold I Had Not Realized,
All The Stories That Were Held Inside No Never Told!
No Longer Are They Buried Within My Pot Of Gold

And Now A Smile May Appear On My Face At Times
For The Day Your Soft Brown Eyes Gazed Into Mine,
Your Beautiful Eyes Took Me To A World Of Heaven!
Sweetly I Go Down The Path Of Our True Love Again!

Forever I Will Wait Though Just Waiting As I Grow Old
For Your Soft Brown Eyes To Look Into Mine Again I Hope,
No Longer Do I Care To Live On If With You It Cannot Be
For Your Eyes Took My Heart And My Soul They Do Keep!

Rose Portillo

The Whisper Of His Soul

The Whisper Of His Soul Lingers In My Heart
In My Sleep It Is Captured So We're Never Apart
Whispering Sound Of His Voice I Hear As I Dream
Along With My Love Causing The Urge To Scream!

The Whisper Of His Soul Steals All Of My Days
Like A Thief Running In The Dark Of The Night
With Each Whispering Soft Kiss Given From Only Him
Memories Staying On My Lips Never Growing Dim

The Whisper Of His Soul Yes Haunting My Nights!
Oh The Longing Of His Touch From His Warm Arms
Taking Me To The Never Ending Deepness In The Dark!
The Torture Of His Sweet Memory Burning Ever Bright

The Whisper Of His Soul Echoes Lonely With Me Still
He's Waiting For Me To Go To Him Yes I Know I Will
While I Wait Living Sadly Miserable Until Then Though
Wonder Why Can't I Leave Now So I Keep Asking When

Now The Whisper Of His Soul Always Comes To My Ears
Each Night With His Spirit Sitting There Closing My Eyes
Inviting Me Taunting Me Telling Me Not To Ever Awake!
I'm Still Here Waiting In Tears Still To This Gnawing Ache!

Rose Portillo

Poison

THE POISON I PUT INSIDE MY BODY EACH DAY
IT IS CAUSING MY ADDICTION FOR I AM ITS PREY

TO EASE ALL THE PAIN THAT LINGERS INSIDE MY VEINS
BUT ONLY CAUSING ADDED PAIN IF IT IS TAKEN AWAY

THE POISON I HATE TO TAKE ITS TOXIC FOR YES I'LL DIE
EITHER WAY I CHOOSE TO LIVE WITH THE PAIN OR MY CRIES

WHAT DO I DO THIS I ASK GOD EVERY DYING DAY
WHY WAS THIS DONE TO ME WHY I WAS JUDGED THIS WAY

I CANNOT LIVE WITH IT NOR CANNOT LIVE WITHOUT
POISON EATING UP MY BODY IT EASES PAIN NO DOUBT

ONLY TO CAUSE MORE PAIN FOR IT CRAVES TO STAY
DECIDING TO TAKE MY BODY NOT HELPING LIVING IN VAIN

ROSE PORTILLO

The Very Sight Of You

At The Very Sight Of You
Made My Heart Stand Still Thrilled

With The Very Sight Of You
The World Vanished No One In My View

And The Very Sight Of You
Makes My Cares And Worries Gone Too

Since The Very Sight Of You
It Kept My Heart It Stole My Soul

But The Very Sight Of You
Made All My Dreams Come True

So The Very Sight Of You
Means Waiting A Lifetime Only For You

Upon The Very Sight Of You
All My Dying Days Make My Nights Blue

Of The Very Sight Of You
Keeps My Heart Beating Ever So True

So The Very Sight Of You
Brings You To Me Even During My Sleep

Then For The Very Sight Of You
Takes Me To Heaven So My Sleep I Keep

Rose Portillo

The Very Breath Of You

The very breath of you and your essence too,
Yes it is what gave me life here once again

The ribbon of your spirit leads only to my soul,
Entwined together so very many lifetimes ago

Tell me how could you ever believe in your heart,
That I could survive my life without you let alone apart

When my sad lonely soul is slowly dying inside,
Suffocating as the breath of you needs every part of me

You are the closest to Heaven that I have ever come,
The spiritual love felt was truly straight from up above

Our spirits were tied and bound from the deep within,
The two golden ribbons of love were connected intensely

Sealing our souls inside one another in the deep inner realms,
Of the beautiful love that only our two souls within now dwell

Rose Portillo

The Rain

The Rain Will Always Seem To Fall
No Matter What We Do To Hope It Docsn't

It Can't Help But Break The Sunny Day
Temptation Induced Much Too Great Is Sought

Just When The Sun Believes It Is Come To Stay
The Rain Brings Her Self Always Along The Way

But What Is Fun For One And Yes For Some
May Be A Great Despair For Us And For The Sun

Rose

The Sweet Pain

The moment I saw your face one thing I knew
The moment you looked into mine you knew it too
I knew you had been mine from even long ago
You'd be mine once more this also had been foretold

Our love was made in the mere Twilight of the Dawn
Made from each other's Spirit's love dwelling among
Our hearts beating as the breath of our souls touch within
Gold And Silver Cords entwined is how our story begins . . .

Could you possibly have known all of the untold
As you still exist in the air I live and still breathe in
The way you looked into my eyes is now about to unfold
How you stole the truth from right out of my inner soul

There is no end to The Sweet Pain that to my heart was sent
Knowing your heart felt the same as to when you began
I tamed your beautiful heart with love still united in mine
Not so truly hidden inside my soul though still so sadly blind

Deep down inside of my lies no longer do you wish to stay
Hiding my love for you can stay a secret no more this way
The Aura of your Spirit's Color shows everywhere in the air
Breathing in your essence waiting knowing you are still here

Though as I walk this earth you cannot heal The Sweet Pain
From your fierce love as I feel you soar the Heavens above
My love still remains as bold for you with no possible gain
I feel your tears they are the dew on my face from your Love

With each breath that I take each day seems harder I must gasp
For the other half of my heart in the air feel only you I still ache
Reaching out feeling you so close when only air is what I grasp
Touching emptiness in the wind so there again my heart breaks

Rose Minu

The Tears Of A Clown

It was not so very long ago
Since that day I looked in your eyes
Way back in the days of you and I

Dwelling in my mind forever though
Seems just like yesterday we were one
No they said I should let you go

It was not you who said goodbye
There was never any mistrust in your eyes
It was I that failed to come back your way

It was the last time that I saw your face
Happiness is all you saw there was no trace
Although love was the part I played in your heart

But my happiness you knew was just a disguise
To let me in your heart again always makes me sigh
What did you see how did you know I played the part . . .

The Tears Of A Clown . . .
Are The Tears Down My Chin

Rose Portillo

The Tale Of Your Crown

Yesterday It Was A Crown You Wore
Though Gladly At Will You Set It Down
Forever Only To Be In Your Love's Arms

Your Royalty Was Brilliantly Adorn
Compared With Love's Urge To Soar
To All Heights With Love's Charms

Today Your Crown Is Still To Be Worn
In Heaven Where You Are At Home
While You Lay Still Inside My Heart

Yes You Are Shining At Heaven's Gates
Spreading Your Wings From High Above
From Divine I Will Always Have Your Love

Rose Portillo

Your Secret Truth

My Soul Rose Higher Than Any Man Could Ever Go
Your Touch Sent Me Where It Had Never Been Known

Your Foolish Lies Spoken By All The Unbearable Woes
Then Sudden Change Brought Me Back Down So Cold

In One Moment Of Time Without Warning Or Haste
Your Haunting Laughter Was Like Thunder And Rain

Like The Lightening You Struck Straight Into My Heart
I Fell Along With The Leaves On The Ground I Lay Apart

Your Smile So Cruel I Saw On Your Face So I Cried
As The Rustle Of The Leaves Whispered Your Secret Inside

Rose Portillo

Your Leaves Fresh And Green

When My Leaves Stay Fresh And Green,
My Trees Budding Are Forever To Be Seen,
Will Only Then Shall You Be Mine Forever?

Your Forever Seems To Be Just For A Little While,
Until My Stems Of Brown Have Then Turned So Pale,
The Ground Can No Longer Bare Your Loving Smile

When There Seems To Be No Beauty Or Loveliness,
My Eyes Will Not Search Any Longer For Your Caress
Inside The Beauty And Riches Under Your Soil Mess

Your Love Seems To Be Only What Shows Of Your View
But Not The Beauty That Is Lying Beneath My Tree Of Dew
And You Can No Longer Have Love For The Thorn Bush

For The Beauty That Lies Is But Of What Does Not Show
To Remember Of The Pretty Flower That Cannot Be Seen
So You Give No More Love You Pretend Of Love's Growth

This is dedicated to someone who forgets to love when times are bad
when there is no smile on my face, this is dedicated to you, the one who thinks he
loves me.

Minu

Sometimes To Find

To Find Knowledge And Wisdom
Sometimes Is To Find Solitude And Pain

And To Find Patience And Grace
At Times Is To Find Sufferings Long

To Find Peace And Mercifulness
Is To Find Undoubtedly Mistakes And Errs

To Find Love, Happiness And Pure Joy In One's Heart
Is To Find Forgiveness In Others As Well Within Yourself

To Find The Greatness Of Pure Love And Final Safe Haven In Life
Is To Finally Find The Divine Greatness Of The Heart And Soul . . .

Always With No Strife

Rose Portillo

To The One I Used To Love

I have this feeling way down deep inside
Something that I realize I should no longer hide
My feelings for you have always been very real
Although you might say to everyone you do not believe

It's not what you say that affects how I feel
It's when I have a ton of problems—on my shoulders
I go to you and when I cry you wipe away my tears
When I'm scared you chase away all of my fears

Every time I have a problem you are always there
And even when I don't you always just seem to care
Late at night while I'm asleep you whisper in my ear
Words I wish a mouth couldn't keep my biggest fear

You whisper "Good-bye" and then stroke my hair
When I open my eyes I don't see you anywhere
My heart falls it breaks this is too much for me to take
It's been a few weeks now so I try to kill the pain

I just don't know how when you don't even call
I guess you don't know how that makes me feel . . . small
Then on a cold Friday afternoon I see you with my best friend
After she told me she won't be back til' June!

It's funny cuz, you told me you'd be there til' the end
Why do I feel so betrayed? It's like my happiness has been delayed!
Now I sit here alone and depressed
Then I think of the expression on your face, not one bit upset

Then she made me feel like I was in the wrong place
Now all I feel is anger toward the people I loved the most
If I've eaten I'm not sure I've lost track of my life
And who I used to be I really need to get back to me

Today I found someone new someone who I could talk to
On my love he taking his toll at night he holds my hand
His name is so simple and sweet his name is Dan
Since you've been gone I put a lock on my heart
And he holds the key because he'll never leave anyone the way you left me

Vanessa Espitia

Today

Today I thought of you
As I usually always do
This time my heart hurt all alone
I remembered you're really gone

Today as I thought of you
I actually saw your face in my mind
Then my heart died all over again
Remembering a coffin found in the end

Today I thought of what I did wrong
As I drove around in my car seeming lost
My soul is nothing but empty inside no song
Wanting to die and go where you have gone

Today as I thought of you My Love
I cried tiring sad lonely forever tears
Again my spirit leaves me blue without you
Only finding with me you will no where be near

Rose Portillo

Twin Souls

Wherever Your Beautiful Soul May Go
Whatever Your Wonderful Soul Will Do,

Whatever Dimension You Have Entered
Whatever Realm You May Have Walked In,

I Feel Your Spirit Right Here Along Side Of Me
Your Soul Is Within Mine To Them You Are Gone,

Your Spirit Has Searched Divine's Truth To Find Me
The Other Part Of Your Soul Reached Inside Underneath

Cosmic Rays Departed Once As Our Birth Together Was Done
Creating The Death Of Two Souls Because Forever We Are One

As Our Lives Played The Other Roles Which The Stars Found
My Soul Entered Your Soul And Inside Of Mine You Belong

Your Love Your Heart Are Mine Always This We Do Know
Waiting For Me The Gnawing Urge With You Together Strong

Where You Are Until I Find You Again My Twin Soul's Song
Your Spirit Within The Essence Is Locked With My Soul Along

Rose Minu

What Happens

What Happens When There Is No More Pain
When There Are No More Tears To Keep You Sane?

Will There Be Any Happiness In Your Heart To Gain
Or Sadness Because The Thrill Is No Longer For You?

Does The Pain You Create In My Life
Assure You That There Is Love For You Still?

Does Seeing The Tears That Fall From My Eyes
Say the Words You've Been Longing To Hear?

Will You Long For The Days Of Pain
And Sorrow For Your Reassurance Again?

Will You Try And Create More So Called Love Just So
You Can Feel The Pain And Suffering From My Tears?

Your So Called Love Created So Many Fears
For That Is All That Is Left From Those Years.

Abused,
Rose Portillo

What Love Is

Loving Someone So Deep In Your Heart
To The Point It Tears Your Soul Apart
You Wonder Where Does Love Originate
Pure Love Is From The Lord For He Has No Hate

Loving Someone Forever Loving Them So Much
To Where Your Insides Are All Just Distraught
Then Becoming So Hateful Filled With Only Pain
Wondering If Love Is Really From Heaven Up Above

For Pure Love Would Never Want You To Hurt So Bad
And Love That Renders The Tearing Of Souls So Tough
Seems To Me That Love Like This Is Not Really Love
For It Begins From Oneself And It Is Conceitedly Sad

All That Is Touched By This Sort Of So Called Love
Seems To Become Broken And Torn To Pieces Enough
All That Seemed Good Finally Becomes Deceit And Greed
So What Is Love If It Hurts Not Really Fulfilling Our Needs?

Rose

When It's Too Hard

When you have to try to hold my hand
When it is not in your cold heart to understand

When you have to try to remember to love me
But you think not because you have to be a man

When it is too hard to even try to be nice
Then I know there can be no chance at all

How can there be any love inside your heart
When it's much too trouble for you to even call

You cannot even pretend to love don't know how
It is evident that there is no love inside your heart

So let's let things be done and leave it alone now
We can both be without so much strife being apart

Anyway all you have done is bring tears to my eyes
When it's too hard to love and treat me as your wife

It's simple to go to her but you know she doesn't care
Whether you come or whether you go so it's there

Rose

You Left Your World

You left your world to be in mine
I guess it was you knowing your time
Of showing how much you love me
To show how strong your love could be

That no more hurt could ever really be
That there was always just only you and me
That to get rid of all the pain of the past and,
To show me all our mistakes were of no need

So you left your world to be in mine . . .

Because our world could not be entwined
Remember all this you left with Forgotten Nots
Our wasted days of love and ignorant pride
Collected memories buried souls getting caught

And you left your world to be in mine . . .

Although our mistakes were forgiven from above
That now only time alone was meant to prove our love,
And all of our loving memories were meant to be felt
For tainted guilt of our strong love could only melt

So you left your world to be in mine . . .

You forgot the ways of all those "Should be's."
You gave up all those "Never will be's" . . .
If only the world and everyone else could see
But Heaven alone would cause them to believe

That you left your world to be in mine . . .

You knew the warning sign that was in your heart
You knew the sadness that had played the part
You saw our love was drowning too much hiding . . .
I know just to save us you left so our love could be shining

So you left your world to be in mine.

Rose Portillo

When You Went Away

When you went off and left far far away
To the far away land where there is no gray

You left me here all alone you left me so blue
You forgot one thing though that I needed you

I know if you had known you were leaving
I know this much you would have taken me too

There's no way you would have left me here
If you knew the pain I was going to endure

So I want you to know I forgive you "My Love"
For leaving me all alone when you went up above

For letting me go for leaving me here so very cold
For I know you didn't know you were going to go

It's so hard since you left everyone is so cruel so mean
When you went away it all seems just like a bad dream

Rose Portillo

Whose Pain Is It Anyway?

Please Tell Me Tell Me Now Whose Pain Is This Anyway?
Why Am I Feeling This Horrible Excruciating Pain For
For Whose Benefit Am I Suffering This Undeniable Score

Do I Suffer For The Gain Of A Miserable Vengeanceful Satan
Does This Pain He Induces On Me For His Favor Or Pleasure
Do I Suffer For The Love Of My Lord For My Undying Worth

What Do I Suffer For Why Do I Feel The Constant Pain That I Do?
Is It For The Gain Of My Soul Reaching Another Level In Life
Am I Paying For The Sins Of The Ignorance Living In Strife?

Does My Pain Make Him Smile Does It Even Make Him Sad?
Why Must I Endure Severe Pain In My Body Feeling So Bad
Will Some Justice Be Gained For My Life To Be For The Better?

Tell Me Now Tell Me True Am I Suffering Because Of You?
Is This Pain I Endure Maybe In The End Will Be For Any Good
Will I Become A Better Person Will I Always Remain Just A Fool

Why Do I Suffer So Much Please Tell Me God Is It For Truth
What Will Become Of Me For My Body Is Tearing At The Seams
The Devil Is Laughing At Me I Know Please Tell Me It's A Dream!

Tell Me My Lord Tell Me Why Can't There Be A Better Way?
Why Must I Suffer So Much With This Searing Pain That I Feel
Whose Pain Am I Enduring It For Whose Pain Is This Anyway?

Take My Life For No More Suffering Would Be Better For Me
For My Skin My Tissues Inside Are Slowly Horribly Tearing Apart
It Is Better Than To Lay In Such Pain The Gnawing The Throbbing

Now Tell Me Now Satan Does It Make You Happy For You To See?
That I Suffer The Way I Do Each Day Every Morning That I'm Enduring
I Hope Maybe Then At Least Someone Is Getting Something From Me

Rose Portillo

Carinioso

To Rose

Yo Tengo Un Amor Mas Carinioso *(I Have A Love That Is Most Sweet)*
Que Palabras No Pueden Desir, Mas Precioso *(More Precious That Words Cannot Say)*

When My Eyes Fall Upon All Your Sweet Beauty
I Think To Myself . . . I Take A Deep Breath
And Hold My Composure . . .

So With My Last Gasping Words,
What I Mean Is That I Love You, Rose . . .

I Relax, I Enjoy, I Admire
I Take It In, I Absorb, I Appreciate

I Am At A Loss For Words,
Any Words Are Not Worthy

To Describe My Most Intimate Feelings
And Thoughts Toward You

From Memo
Written in 2004

You

YOU . . .

YOU STAYED AND CRIED WITH ME ALL THE WHILE
IN THE DARKNESS HOPING IN THE STILL OF THE NIGHT

YOU HELPED MY HEART BELIEVE AGAIN JUST LIKE A CHILD
IN ALL THAT HAD ALREADY BEEN LOST IN MY FRIGHT

YOU TOOK MY HAND AND BROUGHT ME IN FROM THE DEEP
AS I HAD SANK MYSELF FROM HIS GRACE IN FOREVERS KEEP

YOU GAVE MY SOUL BACK TO ME IN THE BRILLIANT LIGHT
THAT THIS UGLY CRUEL WORLD HAD TAKEN WITH ALL OF IT'S
MIGHT

YOU . . .

YOU ARE THE ANGEL OF MY LIFE IN DISGUISE
THAT ROCKS ME TO SLEEP WITH LOVE IN HIS EYES

YOU TOOK ME OFF THE ROAD LEADING TO MY DEATH
YOU GUIDED ME BACK INTO HIS GRACE WITH SWEETNESS

YOU HELD ME IN YOUR ARMS WITH MUCH LOVE STILL UNTOLD
ASKING NOT MUCH IN RETURN FOR TO YOU I WAS GOLD

YOU FORGOT ALL ABOUT YOUR OWN WORRIES AND WOES
YOU GAVE IT ALL TO ME THAT YOUR HEART NOW HOLDS,

YOU . . .

ARE TRULY MY ANGEL IN DISGUISE
THANK YOU FOR LOVING ME
THE WAY THAT YOU DO . . .

I LOVE YOU TWICE

ROSE PORTILLO

You Haunting My Soul

It Is You Haunting My Soul Though I Do Not Fear
To This Day You Don't Leave Me You Stay So Near
They Try To Tell Me What I Did Not Want To Hear
I Do Believe In My Heart It's You That Is Still Here

It Was Your Promise To Stay With Me Even After Death
I Remember Even Though It's Been So Many Years When
You Said You Would Come Back And That I Would Know
You Vowed A Promise That You Would Never Let Me Go

You Even Confessed To Me That He Would Feel You Too
You Swore We Would Never Be Able To Get Rid Of You
Forever And Eternity Is What You Said You Would Stay
We Vowed To Each Other Yes We Both Wanted It That Way

This Promise You Gave Was That You Would Forever Keep
This Promise As We Lay We Made In Both Our Heart's Deep
This Was To Never Leave Me In This Cruel World All Alone
You Vowed You'd Never Leave Me It's You Haunting My Soul

So Now As I Lay Here Begging For You To Return In Tears
I Can Feel You Always Trying To Keep Away All Of My Fears
Now I Know What It Was That You Had Told To The World
That It Is You All Along That It Is Surely You Haunting My Soul!

Rose Portillo

You Can Only Try So Much

When Someone Does Not Want To Give
No Matter How Much You Do Not Take
I Say It Is Not You That Fails To Live
It Is They That Is Trying Not To Be Fake

When You Simply Just Do Right By Someone
But All That You Do Is Not Good Enough
Remember Always When You Have True Love
There Is No Wrong It Should Never Be Rough

When Their Suffering Is Only Showing You
That The Only Suffering Is For You To Do
Remember That Love Should Be Felt From Above
This You Must Know It Is Not You That They Love

True Love Will Never Tire Of Being Kind
Of Understanding Or Forgiving This You Will Find
No Need For Explanation Not Even Reasons Why
But When Someone Loves You All Will Be Fine

When You Have Done All You Can Do
They Still Cannot See The Love Is From You
Remember One Thing Is Straight For Sure
You Can Only Try So Much This Is True

Rose Portillo

You Death

Sinking Deeper And Deeper Inside Of This Endless Pit
Magnetically Pulling The Essence Of My Tender Soul
Can Anyone Resist The Power Of The Black Aura Insisted

Blacker Than Black Deeper Than Deep Inside A Dead Hole
Your Presence Is To Just Take Away My Pain As A Friend
Are You An Evil Creation To Cause More Unjust And Sin

Death Are You Slowly Inch By Inch Just Reeling Me In
With Each Heartache In My Life That Brought So Much Pain
Inside Of My Soul I Feel The Pulling From Your Tight Reins

Tomorrow's Uncertainty Where This Deep Darkness Will Lead
Today's Sorrows Taking Me No Where With So Much Pain To Go
Pulling Of Your Black Cord Takes Me To Your Doom Your Home

Your Black Cord May Be The Silver Lining Leading Me To Heaven
Away From This Cruel Awful Pain That Has Seeped Inside Of My Veins
Giving The Urge To Leave This World Are Filled With Hurtful Days

To Go With You Away From This World Of Pain I Live In I Do Pray
Pain Of My Heart As Well As The Illness That Has Crept In To Stay
I Wait To Die In The End With This Dark Aching I Just Lie Prey

Rose Portillo

You Have Your Meaning

You Have Your Meaning,
As You Can Be My Meaning,
But Then I Have My Meaning,
Which May Not Be Your Meaning

It Is Your Mind,
Interpreting What You Will,
For What I Interpret,
Can Never Be Your Will

And Yes Your Interpretation,
Can Never Be My Will Or
Never Have My Meaning For . . .

You Have Your Meaning,
And I Have Mine.

Minu

My Mask

If I put on my mask I can't be seen!
So here I go I put it over the real me
Now I'm someone you don't even know
Someone who will surely let you go
Without a warning I'll do what I want
I'll give myself something new to flaunt
Try to stop me and I'll stop you
Cuz with this mask Oh I'm someone new
Someone who's not afraid of you and your ways
And I honestly don't care if you go or if you stay
Ha-ha-ha is what I'll say if you tell me you what you want
Tell me you want to stay and I'll tell you the chances you got
None sorry you waited too long
Now all this is, is some dumb retarded love song!

When I take off the mask I'm so ashamed
I can't believe I played the game I played
Why did I push you away? Why did I make you go?
Now I'm sitting here terribly sad and alone
So I put the mask back on and I'm back to smiles
I'm not sitting in depression for a long while
I realize I did it because all you did was hurt me
I ask why it took me so-o long to see
I live the rest of my life with my mask
Then I . . .
I wake up from a horrid dream
And I wake to see you're not next to me
I pack my clothes and leave the door open behind me
I bump into you outside smelling like perfume
I get your ring and throw it at you
Then I leave

Vanessa Espitia (14 years ago)

I lost . . . I gained

Today I lost the Love of My Life
The only thing in the world that I could call mine
Now I walk alone to the place where he lays
The place where all eternity he'll stay
My world has been turned upside down and flipped around
I can still hear you voice all around me, it's loud
It's almost too much for me to bare
Cuz I was Your Light and you were My Air
Now I stand over the stone with your name
I cry and find only myself to blame
How could I let you go?
Deep inside and far outside
I loved you more than you know
I remember all of the smiles and the tears shed
And how at night before we slept you'd kiss my head
I still remember your smell and the way you did your hair
At home alone I feel you almost everywhere
I haven't eaten in days and I always feel cold
I sit and think of our plans
And the way we were gonna sit together and grow old
I remember your ticklish spot and your favorite song
People look at me and tell me you've been here all along
The empty side on the bed
And the trash is never taken out
Lets me know that they don't know what they're talking about
My Soul Mate, My Star, The Reason I smile
I can't help but now just sit in denial
I feel sick My Love I have to go
But I'll be back I won't leave you alone

Today Love, I have good news!
News that strayed me away from the life I used to
I bare inside me the child we made
I wish you could have seen this
I wish you would have stayed
This is my last visit I will start over now

Vanessa Espitia (14 years old)

41

I Believe

I believe!

I believe we can stop Global Warming
I believe we can stop this war from storming
I believe we can feed the starving children
I believe we can bring back our military men

I believe!

I believe in our parents for love and care
I believe we can stop our cars from polluting air
I believe we can put smiles on the homeless
I believe I can help spread happiness

I believe!

I believe that money is a disease widely spread
I believe that fame and glamour leaves you dead
I believe Rock n Roll is an inspiration
I believe music can lead this torn nation

I believe!

I believe if one person will rise we all will
I believe there is hope for the hopeless still
I believe the world can be changed by a teenage girl

All of this belief keeps me alive
Becuz this world and the people running it are living a lie!

Vanessa Espitia
(14 years old)

No Thnx

No thnx I could do without it
What is fame but a sickness too good to contain
It spreads widely n just causes more pain
It turns you backward n lets you go
U'll be confused n blind n not know what you know
Fame is like a cage locked from the outside
While locked inside into the bars you collide
You become numb n unaware of what is being done
Fame is a battle that it itself already won
You have to hide the pain n distress with smiles
And you get dragged in circles for miles and miles
Fame is an uprising of all of your fans
All your fans are bored people with nowhere to stand
To ignorant to see what really goes on
The lines for your fans do nothing but grow long
All you can do is drink, drink, drink
Before you know it you can't think
You are controlled by agents n propaganda
Trapped in a system you can't get grasp of
You soon will turn to pills n rehabilitation
All of this has turned into a bad collaboration
This story ends all to horrid
But fame is a sickness too great too contain
It spreads faster n injects large amounts of shame

Vanessa Espitia

My World Your Lives

My whole world as your mother evolved around your lives
It has been that way since the beginning of all you being born

It's nice to know I have every childhood memory inside stored
All of your smiles your loves all your hurts and all your cries

All that I hold that is deep and true in my heart just for you
If only I took more time to tell you how dear you are to me

I have always loved you so much just right from the start
Even when you hated me with me you always fought so hard

Just remember that my world was all about living just for you
Every moment you lived every breath you took in my heart deeply lies

Now that you are adults and on your own with your own children
I wait for you to call I feel I bother but I always have you in my mind

When I'm gone from here and you think I cannot hear the words you send
When you are just sitting there all alone and you hear a knock at your door

Know this much as you go to open it and you think it's only the wind
It's me knowing I have to go but I'm still hoping you'll invite me in

All I know is the touch of your kisses are still within my heart I miss
Don't forget this when it is in your child's eyes that you have forever been

I do wait for you I miss all the laughter and love we used together share
Because of your other lives I feel not to impose waiting for you to come here

I love you forever even after the day I die for you will always be my children
For you were in my every thought as you grew each moment again and again

Every thing I've done all my life remember all of you are The Light Of My Eyes
I wish you loved me more but if you were not here I would have no reason to live

Rose Portillo
To All My Children From Your Mom

The Games The Devil Plays

On one of the days that my tormenting pain was so severe
I paused a moment crying so hard sitting in a puddle of tears

I asked the devil why with this pain did he play the games he played
Wondering if he would have the *courage* to answer as I *dared* to stay

Knowing damn well everything out of my mouth the devil he does hear
You keep hurting me over and over all the more I love Jesus in return

This I said, "You know all you do is draw me closer to The Lord"
Each time you make me cry all I do is pray harder for God to help me more

"So why, why do you create this awful pain that you cause for me
Why are you playing that hard to win over this game is this ugly reality?"

I want you to know "You will never win I know you must know this by now
Is it that you're not playing to win the game at all at least not for yourself?"

Could it possibly be that you just might be really playing in this game of life
In the strange reality check that you maybe working for the other side after all?

Could it possibly be that closer to the Lord Jesus is what you really want me to be?
Is this so crazy that you are on God's side and this is what you try to get from me?

For I know you know each time you pick on my heart it is not for your name
All I do is Read The Word more than I ever did before are you playing Jesus's
game?

I have a feeling that in this twisted way you may be working for Jesus Christ all
along
For you do not stop and are not happy until I'm back praying to Him in all his
Psalms

If this is your way of trying to win the souls that you need so much so you say
They are not really for you to win but for you to see less years that you'll pay!"

Rose Portillo

45

Your Friends

It never ceases to amaze me
That to this day even with your age

Your friends have so much influence
To make you leave or cause you to stay

I hear it in the things that you do not say
What is said is only half or some of the truth

Letting them say bad things not standing by me
Covering up what they say even if it's rudely

Instead of being good telling them it was you
You let them talk about me making yourself look good

And I know that what I see and with all that I hear
I don't want the kind of man you are with them to be

Because you don't want them to see you're a fool
Sitting there smiling not telling them all along you are

I don't like you anymore or what I hear and what I see
Leave me alone now won't you just please leave me

Stay with your friends be all you portray yourself to be
Yes have your friends and what they want you to see

Rose Portillo

Love At First Sight

It must have taken you such a very long time
Even back then with the other relationships you had too
Comparing you now I know we are not going to make it
I feel right about you not loving me now I must tell you

It was so obvious that we should have just stood friends
I should have followed my instincts right from the start
So different were the ways that you would treat me
Why did I have to tell you how to use your own heart

It hurt so bad at first I needed the time to absorb
All the pain that you caused me why didn't I just leave
It was your lies that I think you even tried to make true
It was hard feeling sorry for me trying not to conceive

Both of us really thought that it was right for us at first
We didn't want to have another failure in our lives
But it wasn't that we were both bad people trying to hurt
It must be that we both believed in Love At First Sight

Rose Portillo

To Say Goodbye

I guess it was something that we both needed to do
To spend the last time together to see if we had love true
What other way were we were supposed to find out about it
If we still have love or is it meant for us to be separated

I am glad that we did it this way at least now we know
This way I felt it for myself and saw the real you again
We gave it a second chance and tried to make a go of it
Now I know our love just didn't drift away with the wind

If we hadn't tried this again or hadn't even bothered
We would forever be wondering whether it was sent from above
The sadness would have overwhelmed me possibly forever
This way we got it over with and no more doubts of our love

So now I could say goodbye without feeling I made a mistake
I could honestly say that I know that we could just be friends
There will be no anger for now I know it is better for us this way
Instead for us to forever be trying and arguing would make no sense

Rose Portillo

Just A Woman

When I Was Just A Woman It Was Only Just About Me
I Was The Best Of Whatever It Was That I Wanted To Be

When I Was The Queen I Gave The Country All Of Me Or Nothing
I Had No Children No Husband That Would Want To Become King

When I Was A Mother It Was What I Wanted Even If I Was Not Free
Children Became All I Did It Was Only What A Mother Should Be

Woman With A Career It Was What I Became All About Those Years
Then I Had No Children So My Career Would Not Have To Share

For When A Woman Tries To Be A Part Of Two Entities Or More
There Will Be One Part Of Her Life That She Will Eventually Abhor

You Can Not Have Two Masters Nor Can You Love Equally Two Men
You Can Either Love One More Than The Other With One Love To Win

If I Want To Be Just A Woman With Anything Else I Have No Guess
I'm Trying To Have The Best Career For Something Else Will Be Less

One Or Most Surely Some Of All Will No Doubt Suffer In The End
There Will Surely Be Lacking One True Love That Cannot Will Not Bend

For A Woman Has Certainly No Business Having Any Children At All
If A Woman Wants To Save The World Having To Let Her Children Fall

How Can I Serve My Country As Well As A Queen To Rule It Completely
For I Share My Heart Hurting Those When I Leave My Motherly Duties

I Will Have To Show My Country Whom I Love So Dear Yes I Do Treasure
With The Death Of My Child No More Than Theirs That Vow Their Life Forever

So If I Choose To Be Just A Woman Maybe A Mom Yes To Have Children
While I'm Trying To Save The World Causing Them More Hurt Than To Be
Alone

If I Was Born To Have Children To Be A Mom Then That Is What I Choose
They Are All I Will Love For Nothing Comes First For Them No One Will Lose

Rose Portillo

The Weeping Willow

DOES THE WEEPING WILLOW LIVE JUST TO REALLY WEEP
DOES SHE JUST SIT WAITING TO HEAR ALL OUR WOES AND CRIES
DOES SHE ANTICIPATE THE PRESENCE OF ALL THOSE IN NEED
SO SHE WILL HAVE SOMEONE SHARING BROKEN DREAMS TO
KEEP

AS SHE HEARS ALL THE SECRETS OF ALL THEIR LOVERS' CREED
MAYBE SHE WEEPS ALONG WITH ALL WHO SHED THEIR TEARS
UNDER HER SHADE OF BEAUTIFUL DEEP SLEEPY LOVE'S LEAVES
SITTING ALONE WAITING FOR YOU TO COME PLAY UNDER HER
SHADE

AS SHE FEELS ALL HEARTS FELTS THAT ARE BROKEN BUT SHARED
SHE CAN'T HELP BUT LAY HER WEEPING BRANCHES AS IF HER
HAIR
AS THE WIND BRUSHES AGAINST HER ALL THE WAY THROUGH
THE WEEPING WILLOW CRIES TO US ALL ABOUT OUR SAD
TRUTHS

FOR ALL THOSE WHO LOVE TO SIT AND LONG TO STAY WITH HER
LISTENING TO HER AS THE SOFT WIND BENDS AND YES AS SHE
SWAYS
YOU WILL HEAR HER WEEPING WILLOWS CRYING OUT AS ALL SHE
BEARS
ALL SECRETS KNOWN TO ONLY HER WHILE LOVERS SHARE THEIR
HURTS

ROSE PORTILLO

My Father And You

My Father the only man who truly loved me so
You took him from me before his time before he had to go
They say that it wasn't You that took him away from me
Everything is of you those who took him is because of You

Then He came into my life he loved me the same way too
Why did you have to take him away to Heaven with You Too?
The only two men in my life I had ever truly loved now gone
No matter what they say I know You will always be the one

I will never be over them for now I am living here all alone
Why when I had asked them over and over again not to let me go
My father I miss him so much I still feel the pain deep within
He was everything I needed he taught me how to believe again

They weren't supposed to go from this world not yet this I know
Why did You have to take them from me and leave me all alone
Is it that You wanted to show me not to love them the way I do?
How am I not supposed to love the way that You taught me to?

How was I supposed to love them they were my life my only dream
They were all that I had in this ugly cruel world they took care of me
How am I supposed to go on this way as if they never existed in my life
How can I pretend it hurts so bad I can't live without them to guide

They say that it was because I loved both of them just a little too much
They say that I wasn't supposed to love or cherish them like that at all
Was I supposed to love only You and nothing else in this ugly life?
Why did you create "Love" for what reason did you make us alive?

But better yet with all of their love they gave I know it came straight from You
Please tell me this with all their love they gave how could I not Love them too?
They loved me lovingly taking care of me isn't that what You wanted them to do?
How could you allow them both to love me so much only to take them with You?

Rose Portillo

How Do I Free My Soul

HOW DO I FREE MY SOUL
AFTER YOU HAVE TAKEN IT FROM ME

HOW DO I FREE MY SOUL
WHEN IT IS CAPTURED WITHIN YOU SO DEEP

IT IS NOT FOR YOU TO HOLD ANY LONGER
FOR YOU HAVE LONG BEEN GONE SINCE THEN

SO HOW CAN I FREE MY SOUL
WHEN YOU ARE THE ONE THAT HAS ITS HOLD

WHO DO I ASK TO RETRIEVE IT NOW
FROM WHERE CAN I GO AND FIND IT AND HOW

HOW CAN I FREE MY SOUL
WHEN YOUR HEART HAS STOLEN IT NOW

PLEASE YOU CAN FREE MY SOUL
YOU ARE THE ONLY ONE ABLE TO RELEASE IT

SO IT IS YOU TO TRY AND FREE MY SOUL
ONLY YOU CAN FOR IT HAS BEEN IN YOUR HANDS

HOW DO YOU FREE MY SOUL NOW
WILL YOU GIVE IT BACK FOR YOU'VE HAD IT SO LONG

HOW DO I FREE MY SOUL FROM YOU
BETTER YET HOW DID YOU TAKE IT FROM WITHIN

YOU DO NOT REALLY WANT TO FREE MY SOUL
HOW DID MY SOUL BECOME ENTWINED WITH YOURS

HOW CAN YOU FREE MY SOUL THEN
GIVE ME THE SECRET THAT HOLDS ME FROM WITHIN

HOW CAN I FREE MY SOUL FROM YOURS
YOU HOLD THE KEY TO THE REALM OF WHERE YOU'RE IN

HOW CAN I FREE MY SOUL AGAIN
THEN MAYBE I WILL FIND MY HEART WHERE IT IS

HOW CAN I FREE MY SOUL NOW WHERE COULD YOU BE
WILL YOU FREE MY SOUL OR THEN JUST COME BACK TO ME

ROSE PORTILLO

In The Clouds

I was high in the clouds once,
Though it was such a long time ago
Such a beautiful sight there was to see
But how was I supposed to know?

It felt as if I was taken right into Heaven,
Of course I was on top of the world
I didn't want to ever come back down
It was all the more I had never been told

Just the clouds alone were such a delight
To be inside of their soft love of billory white
Knowing that not a soul knew much of how it was
Wishing I could fly away just like a beautiful dove

Maybe one day I will be high in the clouds again
Maybe this time I won't have to come back down
I will look down on my loved ones and I will wish
Until they're ready in the clouds that I'll be around

Rose Portillo

He Was My Father

I was so young I still remember "He Was My Father"
I was a child I would follow him all around the house
Watching everything he did and everything he said
He taught me everything all that life was about

It was always about him yes "He Was My Father"
Every day when he would come home from work
I would run so fast just to see his face his loving smile
Hoping he'd help me understand all that was to come

He tried to tell me that not all was going to be fun
He warned me against those that would hurt me inside
I listened to him I heard every word I knew he was right
He was so good I never thought I'd see the day he'd be gone

I thought he would live forever because "He Was My Father!"
He was so strong so intelligent and wise yes so loving and kind
I never saw a man so tough yet that could be so tender and sweet
He had a way about him that could change your sadness to glee

There was so much finesse in everything he did "He Was My Father"
He loved being good to others he didn't know how not to be
He would feed the poor invite them in our home sit with homeless
I wish he were here it's funny it was him that even taught me to be a lady

I love him so very much and still miss all of his loving ways
This is dedicated to "My Father" for there is no other way to be
He was the best he could be even though he was not perfect I know
He was the perfect gentleman to me I never wanted him to leave

Rose Portillo

56

Addicted

BEING ADDICTED TO SOMETHING AGAINST YOUR BEST
KNOWLEDGE
WHAT DO YOU DO WHAT CAN YOU SAY THERE IS A SECRET
ABOUT IT
WHAT DO YOU SAY TO ANYONE THAT FEELS THEY KNOW HOW IT
FEELS
ESPECIALLY WHEN IT IS SOMETHING THAT TAKES AWAY YOUR
ILLS

WHAT WOULD THEY SAY WHAT WOULD THEY DO IN YOUR
SHOES?
WHAT DO THEY THINK OF YOU SO WHAT IF THEY DON'T
UNDERSTAND
YOU KNOW THEY CAN'T MAYBE THEY SHOULD BE IN YOUR PLACE
TOO
UNTIL THEY FEEL YOUR PAIN UNTIL THEY HAVE YOUR HANDS

IT IS SOMETHING YOU CANNOT AND DO NOT HAVE A CHOICE
IF YOU DON'T TAKE THIS DRUG YOU LIVE IN SUCH SEVERE PAIN
EVIL PAIN THAT MAKES YOU NOT SLEEP YOU CANNOT EVEN
THINK
IF YOU TAKE IT YOU SLIP DEEPER INTO THE ABYSS OF BEING
INSANE

INSANE FOR THE MOMENTS THAT ARE NOT WANTED ANYWAY
NO ONE WANTS TO BE STUCK ON SOMETHING THAT TAKES YOUR
LIFE
NO ONE WANTS THEIR BODY TO HURT MORE EVEN OVER JUST A
VICE
WHAT DO YOU DO EITHER WAY YOU ARE IN PAIN CAUSING STRIFE

FOREVER STRUGGLING WITH THE DECISION TO TAKE IT OR NOT
WHAT DO YOU DO TODAY YOUR PAIN DOES NOT LET IT STAY
AWAY
LIVING IN AGONY FROM A DISEASE WITH WHICH YOU WERE
CURSED
IF I DON'T TAKE THE MEDICINE YOU GIVE THROUGHOUT THE
DAY

IF YOU STOP THIS SO CALLED DRUG IT'S A MATTER OF TIME YOU
DIE
WHICH WAY DO YOU WANT WHICH EVIL DO YOU WANT TO STAY
YES YOU JUST WANT TO BE HAPPY YOU JUST WANT TO GET BY
WHO WILL HELP YOU IT'S OKAY THIS DRUG HELPS YOU STAY
ALIVE

Rose Portillo

A Hurt Heart
My Father

When he died he died with such a hurt heart inside
Thirty some years believing in the love of his wife
He knew if she left him though he would die
He had no idea she wanted him out of her life

They say it's such a sad sad way to leave this earth
To leave feeling you are lost but very much alone
It's so good to know that you are loved while alive
Why did he have to die with a hurt heart and so cold

He never tried to hurt anyone or try to be so mean
He loved making people laugh even when he was leaving
How could such a beautiful man be left here so all alone
All he ever wanted was his family always to have to hold

How could they do what they did before his last goodbye
They could have waited one more hour for us to see him alive
Instead they selfishly pulled the plug not caring of anyone else
Knowing he wouldn't see us but we are still living in his heart

How cruel they were they had no right who did they think they were
It was not for them to say the Lord knew they were not in charge
We were in his life too God knows we had the right to see him before
But they took his life anyway so very sad with already "A Hurt Heart"

Rose Portillo

You Told Me

You Told Me I Had Stars In My Eyes
That Was So Very Long Time Ago

You Told Me I Was Your "Angel Eyes"
And You Made Me Love You So

You Rocked Me You Held Me All Night
In The Deep Of The Night I Held You Tight

You Told Me You Wanted To Take Care Of Me
Now He Has Told Me The Same Very Thing

You Told Me To Always Light Your Fire
I Remember This Like It Was Yesterday

You Told Me That You Would Never Leave Me
It's Been Twenty Five Years Where Are You?

You Told Me You Would Have It No Other Way
Well Then Tell Me Why Didn't You Stay . . . Stay?

Why Would You Leave If You Promised Otherwise
I Held Your Love Was I Not Your "Pretty Eyes?"

Rose Portillo

Why Did You Leave?

TELL ME WHY DID YOU REALLY LEAVE ME
WAS IT TO WAKE ME UP FROM THE DEAD?

DID YOU SENSE SOMETHING I NEEDED TO KNOW
WASN'T THERE ANOTHER WAY TO BE TOLD?

TELL ME THEN WHY DID YOU LEAVE ME?
WELL MOST OF ALL THEN WHERE DID YOU GO?

TELL ME WHERE YOU ARE RIGHT AT NOW
ARE YOU SOMEWHERE I WILL BE ABLE TO GO?

DID YOU KNOW THAT I WAS MUCH TOO NAÏVE
I ALWAYS NEEDED SOMETHING FOR YOU TO SHOW

BUT BY YOUR LEAVING ME YES ALL ALONE
WERE YOU TRYING TO SHOW ME HOW TO GROW?

WHY DID YOU LEAVE TELL ME PLEASE?
FOREVER I WILL ASK YOU WHY DID YOU LEAVE?

ROSE PORTILLO

Encircled In Time

Encircled In Time With Atoms And Neutrons
Forever Flowing Entwined Together In Endless Ages
What Becomes Of That Which Is Involved Through Eons
Revolving Lives Energetic Spiritual Stages From Here On

Evolving Around And Around For Many Years To Come
Where Do We End And Where Do We Come From
Does The End Reach Far Only To Begin All Over Again
Returning Always In Ancient Years Back To The End

The Realms And Dimensions Tremendously Are Hundreds More
Each Energetic Entity Inside Finding Others To Combine
The Outcome Astounding Belonging To The Age Of Dawn
Can We Begin Again Our Pasts In Line If That's What We Find?

If This Is True The Realm Plateaus Are Of Endless Ribbons Of Time
That Many Are Forever And Ever But Then Are We Really Alive?
Our Realms Are Here And There Or Are We Really Anywhere?
Existing In Dimensions Of Time In Endless Circles Of Illusion

If All Is In Reality What Is The Reality Are We Encircled In Time?
Than Why Not Begin Again Where We Met So It Will Not End
Also Our Beginning Of Time Is Of Our Own Chosen Dimension Then
If We Decide To See Again Our Spirits In Quest So We Can Begin

Rose Portillo

I Am Not Of This World

Don't They Know
They Should All Just Shut Up

Don't They Know
They All Hurt My Head

Don't They Know
I Am Not Of This World

I Am Not One Of Theirs
They're Inherited Not Bred

Don't They Know
I Am Insane

Don't They Know
I Have Already Lost My Mind

Can't They See
I Am Not Here Yes I Am Gone

For No Longer Am I
Where They Want Me To Be I Had To Go

Rose Portillo

Why Do I Waste My Breath

WHY DO I WASTE MY BREATH,
WHY DO I KEEP TALKING TO THEM?

WHEN I KNOW IT'S ONLY,
ALWAYS GOING TO BACKFIRE ON ME

YOU ARE NOTHING BUT A LIAR,
AND YOU HATE ME I CAN FEEL

WHY DO I WASTE MY TIME,
WITH YOU STILL BY MY SIDE?

WHY DO I KEEP TRYING,
WHEN ALL WE DO IS FIGHT

PERHAPS I NEED TO FORGET
WHAT I CAN'T HELP BUT REMEMBER

HOW CAN I LET GO
WHEN IT WAS ALL I EVER HAD?

ROSE PORTILLO

So Much Hate

I AM FILLED WITH SO MUCH HATE,
I DON'T KNOW WHERE IT COMES FROM

WHY DO I HATE ALL OF YOU PEOPLE,
WHAT DID YOU DO TO ME?

WHY DID YOU TREAT ME SO BAD,
WHY DO YOU HURT ME SO MUCH?

SHOULD I FORGIVE YOU NOW,
WHAT I CAN'T EVEN UNDERSTAND?

MAYBE IF I KNEW WHY YOU DO WHAT YOU DO,
MAYBE THEN I COULD FORGIVE YOUR HAND

HOW DID IT GET SO BAD,
WHY DID YOU TURN ON ME LIKE THAT?

NOW ALL I HAVE IS MEMORIES I HATE
ALL THAT WE HAD SEEMS TO BE GONE SO SAD

ROSE PORTILLO

What If I'm Not Really Here

WHAT IF I'M NOT REALLY HERE AT ALL
IF OUR WORLDS ARE PRETENSE AND MADE UP

WHAT IF WE ARE ALL JUST PUPPETS IN A PLAY
IF THIS LIFE IS FAKE AND IT'S SOME KIND OF JOKE

WHAT IF ME BEING HERE IN THIS WORLD
IS REALLY THAT I AM NOT EVEN HERE AT ALL

WHAT IF YOU DIDN'T JUST DISSOLVE
AND IF YOU ARE ACTUALLY HERE SOMEWHERE

WHAT IF I WAITED LONG ENOUGH TO FEEL YOU
MAYBE THEN OUR TWO WORLDS CAN COLLIDE

WHAT IF THE FUTURE AND THE PAST
WILL BE OF THE END WHEN IT'S ALL COMBINED

WHERE ARE WE WHO ARE WE
DO WE EVEN REALLY EXIST HERE AT ALL?

ROSE PORTILLO

There's A Hole

THERE'S A HOLE INSIDE MY BODY
FOR I AM NO LONGER COMPLETE

DON'T REMEMBER WHAT HAPPENED
SOMEONE SHOT ME OPENED ME UP TO BLEED

I DON'T REALLY KNOW HOW TO FEEL
OR IF I FEEL ANYTHING ANYMORE AT ALL

BUT SOMETHING DOESN'T LET ME CARE
NOTHING MATTERS TO ME BUT WHERE YOU ARE

BECAUSE WHEN YOU LEFT ME ALL ALONE HERE
YOU LEFT INSIDE OF ME A DEEP HOLE SO BARE

NO ONE WILL EVER BE ABLE TO FILL IT
NEVER AGAIN WILL ANYONE BE ABLE TO COMPETE

YOU CAN'T EVEN SEE THE BOTTOM
FOR IT IS TOO DARK AND MUCH TOO DEEP

THERE'S A HOLE INSIDE OF ME
THAT IS TOO HOLLOW FOR ANYONE DARE TO SEE

THEY WILL NEVER EVEN TRY TO GO INSIDE
FOR SOMETHING IS GONE NOT EVEN I CANNOT FIND

ROSE PORTILLO

So Sad

IT IS SO SAD THAT ALL OF WHAT HAS HAPPENED HAS
BUT TO KNOW THAT IN THIS LIFE THIS TOO WILL PASS

IT WILL ALL JUST GO AWAY WHILE WE TRY TO STAY ALIVE
IT GOES ALL THE WAY THROUGH THEN IT JUST PASSES BY

CAUSING OUR SKINS TO CRAWL AND ALL OUR SOULS TO CRY
SO EERIE THAT IT HAS GONE WE WON'T EVEN KNOW WHY

MY HEART IS SO SAD ALL THE TIME THAT IT HURTS SO MUCH
FOR HOW I FEEL IS SOMETHING I CAN'T EVEN COMPREHEND

WHY THE PERSON THAT I USED TO BE AND HOW NOW I PRETEND
SO WHY DID SHE HAVE TO LEAVE SHE'S GONE TELL ME WHY

THEN THERE'S THE FEELING OF WANTING TO GO BACK IN TIME
TAKING MY SOUL FROM ME IS ALL I FEEL AS I SLEEP AT NIGHT

IS THIS ALL THAT THERE IS ABOUT US AND ALL OF OUR LIVES
IS THIS JUST A DREAM IS IT A NIGHTMARE THAT WE JUST
PERCEIVE

ARE WE IN HELL HERE ON EARTH IS THIS OUR PENANCE TO BEAR
IS THIS PAY BACK WE HAVE FOR ALL THE BAD THAT WE WEAR

WHY DOES THIS LIFETIME THAT WE LIVE HAVE TO BE SO SAD
WHY DO WE SUFFER HERE IT SEEMS ALL ALONE THEN WE JUST
DIE

TELL ME WHAT DO WE DO TO MAKE ALL THE SADNESS END
MAKE DEATH GO AWAY STOP OUR SORROWS AND US FROM BEING
DEAD

DOES ANYONE REALLY CARE WHAT ANYONE DOES ANYWAY
WHERE DO WE END IN OUR LIVES AS WE FINALLY LIE DOWN IN
BED

ROSE PORTILLO

The Stranger

I still walk past the house where we used to live
Wondering why you left me here so alone it's so cold

I ask why I am the only one that is still suffering here though
Breathing the air that we both once breathed ever so bold

Why do I keep breathing knowing you are buried somewhere
Why didn't they take me too wherever you are I want to go there

This life just keeps going on for me endlessly forever without end
Everyone keeps moving as I am suffering knowing you are dead

How sometimes it hurts so bad wishing I could go let me disappear
So weary and tired of it all still wishing that you could still be here

So now what am I going to do without you I'm here so all alone?
I feel like a stranger to everyone what was once my happy home

I'm waiting for you to come back for me so you can take me home
Yet I'm so scared not knowing where it is you want me to go

Rose Portillo

Feeling Lost

I've got that lost feeling that I always get when I think of you
Am I ever going to see you again without you I will forever lose

I try to feel like leaving now I want so much to just go home
I walk home then I remember I can't remember just where to go

So many secrets I held and now are left here with so much untold
Lying down under the sod for with you the lies went deep beneath

My lost love for you never told so we will reap what we sow
They say you're dead why do I still feel lingering here I feel your soul

I know that everything we once had comes to me to stay everywhere
Through your essence of our love your spirit what's left of the truth

My lies have told the secret of who you were but they don't really care
You're telling the world of our love as you exist for me in the air

As they find out the truth from your spirit that lies afloat in the sky
Everything was told to the world through all the unforgotten lies

I will never be able to have the revealing truth of the love of you and I
Yet becoming so much a stranger to even myself so much I can't even cry

Because of all that we had it had to be told to repair all the wrong
The needed lies were brought out from our love existing still strong

I still can't explain how I'm feeling all the more alone and forever lost
I can't find you though in this world all you did was leave me all alone

I should learn how to say goodbye now I know just so that I won't cry
How could I let go when you are so kneaded inside of my sighs?

Rose Portillo

He Was Her Sun

HE WAS HER SUN
SHE WAS HIS MOON
HE COULDN'T GIVE HER
ALL SHE NEEDED TO EXIST

THE MOON TOLD HER SUN
SHE NEEDED TO LEAVE
SO SHE LEFT DESPITE HOW
HE HAD ALWAYS BEGUN

THE SUN TOLD THE MOON
HE WOULD ALWAYS LOVE HER
EVEN THOUGH HOW MUCH
SHE NEEDED TO BE FREE

BUT THE MOON CONFESSED
SHE NEEDED TO SEE THE STARS
AND HER FOREVER LOVE FOR HIM
HAD TO STAY FROM AFAR

SO SHE LEFT THE SUN
TO GO TO STAY WITH THE STARS
THE SUN HE SHINES AS HE WAITS
FOR HIS LOVE IS UNBARRED

HE SWORE SHE WOULD COME BACK
TO HIM HE HOPED ONE DAY SOON
BUT AS EACH DAY HE WAITS
IN THE HIGH BLUES FOR HIS MOON

STILL THERE SHE LIES EVERY NIGHT
LIT AMONGST THE DARK SKY
AS EACH DAY THE SUN DIES WAITING
FOR HIS LOVE TO RETURN ON HIGH

FOR THE SUN LOVED HER SO MUCH
AS HE VOWED HE WOULD DIE
SO DYING OVER AND OVER AGAIN
EACH DAY EVEN AS HE SHINES

HER HAPPINESS IS WHAT HE WANTED
FOR HER THE MOST
SO HE LET HER LEAVE HIS SIDE
TO JOIN THE STARS IN THE DARK SKY

AS THE SUN GOES DOWN
AS EACH END OF HIS LONG WAITING DAYS
SHE RETURNS TRYING TO SEE HIM
TO WATCH HIM DIE IN HER NIGHTS

ROSE PORTILLO

Am I Here

AM I HERE OR AM I IN A DREAM
AM I REAL OR AM I JUST A SCHEME

I FEEL LOST EVEN TO MYSELF I'M A STRANGER
FOR YOU LEFT IN ANOTHER WORLD SOMEWHERE

OR DID YOU JUST FADE AWAY INTO THIN AIR
YET I PRETEND THAT I'LL SEE YOU ONCE AGAIN

IS THIS MY OWN HELL THAT I KNEW I'D CREATE
OR IS THIS MY OWN MADE UP REALITY CHECK PHASE

WHEN WILL ALL OF THIS SADNESS INSIDE OF ME END
WILL I EVER REALLY SEE YOUR FACE AGAIN?

TOMORROW ALWAYS SEEMS SO HORRIBLY CRUEL
TODAY CRYING FOR IT IS SIMPLY MY LIVING HELL TOO

MY DREAMS MY HOPES MAKE ME SUCH A LIVING FOOL
FOR ONLY YESTERDAY IT WAS MY HEAVEN'S RULE

ROSE PORTILLO

Stuck

I FEEL STUCK HERE SOMEWHERE SO TIGHT I JUST FROZE
I'M UNABLE TO MOVE WITH NO HELP I'M SO ALL ALONE

YOU LEFT ME HERE IN THIS STRANGE CRUEL WORLD
RIGHT IN THE MIDST OF THE EYE OF A CRAZY MEAN STORM

I CAN'T MOVE INSIDE THIS PLACE IT SEEMS SO COLD
I CAN'T BREATHE IT HURTS SO DEEP INSIDE MY BONES

I HATE ALL OF YOU! FOR NOT CARING ABOUT ME AT ALL
BUT I LOVE EVERYONE! FOR THIS I KNEW WOULD BE MY FALL

IT ALL SEEMS SO ENDLESSLY SO TERRIBLY MEAN AND CRUEL
IT IS HORRIBLY HOPELESS TO STILL BELIEVE AND WAIT FOR YOU

LIVING THIS LIFE SEEMS TO BE IN VAIN ALL FOR NOTHING TRUE
SITTING CONTEMPLATING MY DEATH JUST SO I CAN GO WITH
YOU

TAKE ME FROM THIS PAIN INSIDE SO FAR AWAY FROM IT ALL
WILL YOU COME TAKE ME NOW PLEASE BEFORE I LET MYSELF
FALL

DON'T KNOW WHERE I AM THOUGH OR EVEN WHERE I CAME
FROM
TRYING TO GO SOMEWHERE TO FINALLY FIND THE END OF MY
PLAN

I'VE LOOKED FOR YOU EVERYWHERE AS I'M TRYING TO PRETEND
STILL ACTING AS IF I HAVE YOUR LOVE HERE WITH ME AGAIN

I HATE YOU! I HATE MYSELF! I LOVE YOU TO THIS VERY DAY
FOR HOW IGNORANT AND WRONG I SIMPLY HAVE ALWAYS BEEN

YOU WERE ALWAYS SO MUCH THE LIGHT THE LOVE OF MY HEART
YOU WERE ALL THAT I NEEDED JUST TO EXIST IN MY LIFE

BUT YOU'RE BURIED! I'M FEELING STUCK WHERE IT'S SO DARK
IF ONLY YOU COULD TELL ME WHERE IT IS YOU DO EXIST

PLEASE COME TRY TO FIND ME! IT'S REALLY ME ALL ALONE
BURIED!
SEE I'M LOST IN THIS DARKNESS! I CANT FIND MYSELF I'M GONE!

ROSE PORTILLO

That Night In Heaven

THAT NIGHT . . .
I THANKED GOD FOR GIVING HIM TO ME AND BEING ALIVE
FOR GIVING ME THE CHANCE JUST TO BE TOGETHER AGAIN

TO BE IN HIS BEAUTIFUL PRECIOUS LOVING ARMS
FOR GIVING ME ONE MORE TIME TO FEEL HOW HE LOVED ME

THAT NIGHT . . .
I FELT AS IF I HAD DIED AND GONE TO HEAVEN WHEN
I ASKED HIM IF THIS WAS REAL WERE WE TRULY HERE

THAT NIGHT . . .
I FINALLY FELT THE TRUE FEELING OF A PEACEFUL LOVING
AND WHAT IT WOULD FEEL LIKE TO BE IN HEAVEN'S BLISS

EVEN THAT NIGHT . . .
I HAD NEVER FELT HIM TOUCH ME WITH SO MUCH LOVE
I HAD NOT NEVER KNOWN WHAT TRUE LOVE FELT TILL THEN

BUT THAT NIGHT . . .
I THANKED GOD FOR ALLOWING ME TO LOVE HIM
TO BE LOVED THE WAY THAT COULD ONLY COME FROM ABOVE

FOR THAT NIGHT . . .
I ALSO FELT THE COLDNESS AND THE LONELINESS
AS IF THE END OF THE WORLD WAS COMING BACK THEN

AND THAT NIGHT . . .
I CRIED SO HARD TRYING NOT TO LET HIM SEE ME FRET
THE TEARS STREAMING DOWN TRYING TO SMILE INSTEAD

FOR THAT NIGHT . . .
I KNEW IN MY HEART THAT GOD HAD GIVEN ME
JUST ONLY ONE MORE CHANCE IN HEAVEN WITH HIM AGAIN

YES THAT NIGHT . . .
I KNEW IN MY HEART THAT NIGHT THAT I WOULD NEVER SEE
THAT IT WAS THE LAST TIME I WAS GOING TO SEE HIS FACE

THAT NIGHT . . .
AS I SILENTLY CRIED AND I WATCHED HIM GO TO SLEEP
PRAYING TO GOD TO TAKE ME AND TO LET ME TAKE HIS PLACE

BUT THAT NIGHT . . .
I ALSO THANKED GOD FOR ALLOWING ME AS I KNEW HE'D LEAVE
TO GO TO HEAVEN ONCE WITH THE ONE HE CHOSE FOR ME

AFTER THAT NIGHT . . .
I LOOKED IN HIS EYES THAT VERY SAD DAY I FELT I COULDN'T
ERASE
I KNEW I WOULD NEVER AGAIN GET TO LOVE HIM THAT WAY

ROSE PORTILLO

A Poem For You:

One Day So Very Long Ago If You Must Know
I Remember You So Much You Were A Young Bo

A Touch On My Lips Seeming But Only For A Moment
I Really Had You Just A Second And Not Much More

Sweet And Tender Though Your Kiss My Love To Unfold
Feeling So Good To Sit Here Now I'm The One Who Knows

Wishing You To Come Home Again Never Wanting You To Go
Pretending So I Would Sit There Near You Beside Your Door

Tell Me Dearest Heart Of Mine Send To Me My Memory Of Old
Do You My Ghost Still Love Me Through All This Suffering Time?

With Your Special Kiss I Still Can Feel You're So Heavenly Still
Knowing Our Special Love When We Were Young Was Such A Thrill!

Rose Portillo

All Too Clear

Once Again I Know This Is All Too Clear
The Purpose Of What I Have To Endure
Though They Were Trials That I Could Not Bear
My Injury Not Passed You Must Know For Sure

Never Easy Not Even When It Was Over And Done
Passing Through Hot Coals Unavoidably Getting Burned
Through Endless Turmoils That Will Never Really Be Gone
As The Channels Of My Soul Have Defeatedly Learned

The Pangs Of Every Tribulation And Continuing To Stay
No Difference Whether From Heaven Or From Astray
Pain Of Each One Of Them That Will Never Go Away
All That Is Here Still Is All That Should Still Remain

Always Craving Urge To Reach You The Silence Is Unknown
Still Seeking To Find Whatever It Was That Had Not Been Told
In The Darkness I Am To Be Haunted By Your Ghost Forever
Of The Memories Of You And Of What Will Never More Unfold

Rose Portillo

Ever Since I Can Remember When

Ever Since I Can Remember When
There Has Been Such A Deep Hole Within
Never Being Filled Although They Tried Hard
Nothing Anyone Could Ever Do Not Even Then

Many Have Come Around Attempting All Along
Many Thought They Could That They Were The One
None Could Compare Or Ever Could Sing Me Your Song
For My Heart Forever Crying For In Your Heart I Belong

This Hole In My Heart I Have Always Felt Even As Young
You Were The Only One Who Unfolded Love Being Real
No More Was Needed Yes It Was You Who Filled It Up
Why Now Then Did You Leave To The Heavens Above

The Hole In My Heart Became Deeper Ever So Bold
Years Have Passed Since That Sad Leaving Time Of Old
No One Could Repair No Matter How They've Tried Still
Trying To Mend Holes In My Heart But Only You Could Fill

Now Feeling Sadness All These Years That Have Gone By
Still Waiting For Someone To Hold Hoping You Are Alive
Trying To Accept That You My Love Again Will I Ever Find
They Said He'll Come Back But He Suddenly Has Arrived

He Wants Me He Loves Me Just Like You Have Done
I Thought It Would Be Good Enough Maybe Just For Fun
He Takes My Mind From Your Love He Helps Me Forget
More So He Fills My Heart With Love With No Regrets

The Love He Gives Me Is So Much The Way You Would
He Says Things You Said It Is As If Maybe You Sent It There
Hard Accepting That It's Still Not You Bringing Me To Tears
But He Loves Me So Much It's As If You Are Still Here

Tell Me You Sent Him For What That No One Else Could
So I Could Stop Crying Now That It's Okay I Love You Still
I Feel Loved By Him I Want You Though To Make Me Feel Good
I Do Think Of Him Too I Hope You Are Not Angry That I Do

So Sorry Love I Don't Mean To Forget Of Me And You
But When He Loves Me That Special Way I Do Feel Brand New
All I Ever Wanted Is You Still But Okay Let Him Love Me True
For Is The Hole In My Heart Filled Up Once Again? . . .

Rose Minu

I Want To Go To Sleep Now

I Want To Go To Sleep Now
I'm So So Very Tired
I Want To Go Home Now
I'm So Lonely And It's Cold

You Don't Know How It Feels
To Wake Up Every Morning
With Gnawing Throbbing Stabbing Pain
Taking Control Of Your Soul Hurting Your Body

Controls Your Every Thought Ruling Your Every Move
It Robs Me Each And Every Day
It Takes Away My Joy Stealing My Happiness Away
Destroying My Urge To Sing Dance And Laugh

You Know I Don't Sing Anymore?
I've Been Singing Since I Was Born
You Know I Don't Dance Anymore?
I Would Dance Everywhere I Would Go

You Know I Don't Laugh Anymore?
Suddenly It's Just Not Funny
You Know I Don't Smile Anymore?
It Hurts Too Much To Smile

I Can't See The Reason That I Need To Stay
I'm More Of A Problem Anyway
I Can't Find The Reason To Still Be Here
I Can't The Pain Just Keeps Getting In The Way

Rose Minu

It's You Again

There You Are Yes It's You Again!
I See I Feel You Even If Only For A Moment
Though I Know It's You Who Comes To Me
I Shed Tears Not Revealing The Truth For Me

When I'm Awake I Feel The Empty Space Of Eternity
It Lies There Stagnant Between Our Two Soaring Souls
As Each Night As I Lay My Head To Keep Your Dream
It's You I Wait To See The Throbbing Of My Heart Knows

No One Dares To Question The Fear Of The Unknown
For There Is Someone Who Still Is Haunting My Very Soul
I Wait For You My Love In All My Sleepless Night Woes
Even In My Sleep I Know That The Truth Shall Be Told

Although The Unknown Still Continues In My Head To Play
In All The Dimensions Of My Mind All Those Nights And Days
I Ask Where Do I Go When I Finally Get To Sleep On By
To The Depths Of Ever Searching For You As Each Sigh

So Now They All Know That It Is True My Love
That It Is You Left Here Seeking My Love From Above
Easing The Deep Pain In My Aching Heart Please Do Tell
The Torture While I'm Awake In This Very Living Hell

Until The Yearning For You Of My Soul Goes
To Escape My Forever Lifetime Daily Misgiven Sorrows
That The Sin Of My Love For You Has Already Sown
Leaving Me Traces Of Guilt For You Left Being Alone

You Are Taking Me As I Sleep For It Is What I Pray
Knowing I Might Wake Tomorrow Only In Pain
To Find Myself Without You In Tears Once Again
So The Truth Is That In My Sleep I Want To Stay

Rose Portillo

Stolen Moments

Stolen Moments With Someone Like You
Is The Love That We Feel Really Real?

You Wish To Stay For Only Just A Moment
Is Your Heart True Is It Really Heaven Sent?

You Know You're Dealing With Someone's Heart
Does It Matter Or Will You Just Play The Part?

It's A Special Thing Only If You Want It To Be
For I Know I Have Loved You But You Can't See?

It's Gone With The Wind As You Always Leave
Playing All The Songs And Pretending As I Sing

It's Okay Though That You Think I'm A Fool
Eventually You Too Will Answer To The Rules

Minu

Sad Sad Darkness

As I Endlessly Sit In This Sad Sad Darkness
What Seems Eternity Certainly Not Sent From Above

On What Seemed To Be The Darkest Night Of All
There You Stood Silently Crying Out For Our Love

You Invited Me To Stay Yes I Heard Your Silent Call
I Saw You From The Heavens I Knew You Had A Fall

It Was So Dark From Where I Was That I Couldn't See
I Felt You There Yes Somehow Quietly Searching For Me

I Found Your Heart Sent From The Heavens Who Set You Free
On The Deep Darkest Night Of All You Were Always Inside Of Me

The Sad Sad Darkness Never Ending Now I Know They Cannot See
Growing Forever Stronger Planting In My Heart Just Like A Seed

So I Find You Each Every Night From My Lonely Deep Sleep
I Reach Into The Sad Sad Darkness Where I Choose For You I Keep

Rose Minu

Too Hard

When You Have To Try Too Hard Just To Hold My Hand
Sad For I Know Now That It Has Never Been In Your Heart

When You Have To Try Too Hard Just To Love A Little
Then You Think You Have To Be A Man To Only Belittle

When It Is Too Hard When It Is Never Easy To Smile
You And I Know There's Been No Chance All The While

We Realize There Could Never Have Been Any Love Inside
Your Cold Stance Has Always Just Shown Deep In Your Eyes

Your Pretense To Love Me Is So Evident To All To Be Seen
Your Heart Is Cold As Ice But You Shouldn't Be So Mean

Leave It Well Enough Alone Now For We Both Do Not Need
The Added Pain And Strife It's Too Hard Not To Be Seen

It Only Brings Tears Along Putting Them In Everyone's Eyes
When It Is Too Hard For You And It Always Only I That Tries

From Rose

You Touched My Heart

You Touched My Heart With Your Smile So Nice
Your Love Seeped In Setting In My Soul Deep Inside

You Touched My Heart And All It's Desire
Your Arms Held Me As I Walked Through The Fire

And Your Tender Kisses Thrilled My Heart Despite
Like The Universe Your Love Caused My Spirit To Rise

I Wait For The Day The Angels Bring You Back To Me
Until Then My Heart And Soul Will Never Be Free

On That Day When The Heavens Opened It's Great Doors
Wonder Where The Angel That With You He Took My Heart

Killing Me Softly Each Moment Your Smile I Pray To See
As I Lay My Head Down To Sleep And Yes Aside To Die I Plea

Rose

Don't They Know?

Don't they know it is you I have always loved,
That our two souls have simply have existed as one
My heart will be crying forever and forever more,
While I go searching for your soul wherever you are

Don't they know who we were and where we've been,
That all the love we had so true is all we have lived?
That since you have left me in this world that I am in,
My broken heart is all alone now and has been ever since

Don't they know that being together is our destiny,
That our souls being apart is the curse we have to feel?
We knew our love was there even before we grew to be,
There is nothing but sweet love between our spirits so real

Don't they see that we know that no one but us is to blame,
That our errs and mistakes have so much become our shame?
Though our love for each other is entwined into never forget,
As we prayed together to be as one forever will it ever be again?

Don't they know each lifetime the whole truth will surely unfold,
We have loved each other before and that it will finally be told
That forever we will soar the universe until we leave this world,
Our spirits along with Our Love is Our Treasure and Our Gold

Don't they know this love between us is forever and eternity still,
That for us there is no ending and no dividing will ever again be?
For us in our next lifetime there will forever be able to see,
That our spirits belong together finally together we'll be free!

Our Forever Love is . . . Forever Above
Don't They Know?

Rose Portillo

In My Sleep

Here You Are My Love You Are Always In My Sleep
I See You But Only For A Moment Yes In My Sleep
Who Is To Know It Is You Though Who Comes To Me
In My Tears Of All The Years Revealing The Truth To Be

Inside In Between You In The Empty Space Of All Eternity
Your Spirit Lies Entwined With Mine We Are A Forever Entity
As Each Night I Lay My Head Down Praying For You To Keep
Waking Only To The Sadness The Sobbing Of My Heart So Deep

No One Questions For No One Really Cares Or Wants To Know
There Is Definitely Someone Though That Is Haunting My Soul
Tell Them It Is You, My One And Only Love, In My Royal Hold
Only In My Sleep I Know That The Truth Shall Finally Be Told

Although While In My Sleep Horrible Unknown Continues To Play
Dimensions Of Space Are In My Mind How Can They Really Say
Where Can I Go Searching For You Tell Me As I Close My Eyes
Maybe To The Depths Of Forever Your Love Is Still Inside My Sighs

So Now They All Must Know It Must Be You In My Sleep My Love
Left Here Alone Only To Fulfill Your Promise Hanging Up From Above
Find Me Again My Heart With Pain Is Still Within, Me Forever Dwells
Torture As I Wake, Finding I'm Still Here Without You Living In This Hell

For The Yearning And Tearing Of My Soul Can Really Be Done
Always Trying To Escape This Life Alone With All My Love Woes
All The Pain Your Love Has Brought Me With Tears I Have Sown
Guilt That I Bear Will Be Forever Among Us For Leaving You Alone

Take Me With You In My Sleep Take Me Is What I Constantly Pray
Fearing When I Wake To Find You Not Here With Me Yet Another Day
Still Here Without You Only With More Tears Knowing I Can Never Gain
I Beg Of You! In My Sleep, Please Take Me Just Don't Let Me Stay

Rose Portillo

It'll Never Be Over For Me

That day as she entered my soul with her smiling glance;
Enchanting me in my head as she whirled in her beautiful dance
I knew right then there was no turning back I would make her mine;
As she spinned so gracefully into my world I was lost in her trance,

I Remember staring, looking in her deep beautiful red-brown eyes;
While I lay across her long reddish hair in all those lovely nights
Holding me oh so near her heart, she knew to lose her, I couldn't bear
So I swore to her, to my death, to never go, not holding any fear

I knew Always and Frever, "It Would Never Be Over For Me;"
I could never leave, our hearts were entwined we would never part
I also promised if she left I would find her any place, anywhere;
For this I knew inside my soul, I would always carry her in my heart

I tried to find her I looked everywhere before the day that I died;
As I lay my soul down that night I entered her spirit while she cried
Where did she go then while I entered her soul with her heart why?
I knew all her tears were for me still lingering a forever long sigh

There she was not ever knowing, no where to be found, until then;
I am searching for her I searched everywhere I felt she may be
Just you all watch and see, I say this forever still, this is my plea;
Baby I'm for real as I told her so, "It Will Never Be Over For Me"

When she pleaded with me that night for me not to go and to forever stay;
I promised to never leave her alone, I said I would never ever go away
My vow I gave her with that very special loving entangling entwined kiss;
And my promise still lies there for her even still in my stolen away death

It's been so many years in between that day and even still until now;
With her tears overflowing in the day and nights of terror of my yoke
She is still remembering on the day of my vow of what I had forever spoke;
For that promise to this day, she does not know I truly have never broke

I'm still here, but why can't she feel me, why doesn't she know?
Just sitting beside her, watching her, she always stays inside of my soul
I wait for her to talk to me, to notice me and to sing to me once more;
Though I have found her now and they will all know that it is so

I entered her soul that day of grief someone tell her I have never left!
There is no me without her for she is in all of my long distant ways
When she sleeps I come, I steal her away I take her from her tortured days
While in her tears, always flowing forever, for what she doesn't know yet

For she still waits for me but still not able to feel me beside her still;
If only she would realize yes I wish she could see I really do hold her tight
Know that I will always be here Always and Forever in the still of the night;
I will come and take her away from her fears, as Destiny Of Our Loving Fate wills

"For It Will Never Be Over For Me" . . . Rose Portillo

I Ask Of You

Why did you leave me here all alone in this ugly cruel world
"My Love" without your smile and love you showed me each day

This I cry to you up above . . .

Why though do I feel the warmth of your body next to mine
As I still long for your touch and your face to see "My Love?"

This I ask of thee from up above . . .

Why do people tell me I must let you go to be happy now?
But I rather keep hanging on to your memories, you know?

This I pray to you from up above . . .

Why when we prayed to every part of our loving vow, I am
Left here in dread with memories of loving you, you're not dead

This I ask you Lord from up above . . .

Why the memory of our love, I rather keep than let go
For to be gone completely I will lose all of my control

This I pray forever and ask Thee instead . . .

Why does no one care or feel because they will never know
That my heart is dying I will forever carry this dreadful toll?

This I ak The Lord from my soul . . .

Why in search of you I will forever more roam
The spark of your spirit to ignite the path I come from

This I ask thee if it is true you are gone . . .

Why do I still wait for you to find me and come knocking at my door
To take me home with you wherever your soul lies, wherever we go,

This I ask of your heart forever more . . .

Rose Portillo

Killing You Softly

You Were The Most Beautiful One In My Life
My First And Most Wonderful Love Ever Lived
Each Night I Still Pray Just to See Your Face
One More Chance To See You Just One More Day

Wishing For Just One More Time To Be By Your Side
Making Sure It Was Me In Your Dreams That One Day
With Tears Still Crying Over The Little Time You Stayed
The Most Beautiful Time Me Ever Knowing This Way

Remembering The Dread Feeling Of The Day It Would End
Knowing In My Heart I Would Always Have To Pretend
For Me You Existed I Know Only For Me And You To Be
For Me You Died Connected So Young I Died Too You See

These Years I Will Always Cherish For Us Ever So True
They Are Not Gone To Me They Only Went With You
Though They Live On As My Tears Are Still Ever So Fresh
My Memories Too Live On Without Any Relief Or Quench

The Guilt I Feel For Going Away Leaving You Alone So Far
Making You Worry Hurting So Bad Stays Deep In My Heart
For I Was Always Just Simply Killing You Softly Deep Inside
Knowing All Of Them Helped In The Keeping Us Apart

I Love You Still . . . Forgive Me I Beg Of You So True
Come Back To Me! . . . Though I Know You Will Never Will
Our Souls Were So Deeply Tied Together So Unbroken Still
The Bond That Made Us One Will Never Be Understood

Killing You Softly Forgive Me For I Never Really Knew
All I Put You Through "My Love" Yes I Was Killing You
More Than I Realized The Death Of Me Was Inevitable Too
I Killed Me Too For I Was And Still Am The Biggest Fool

Rose Portillo

His Smile

Back in the day of me and him so well it wasn't told
How he would always love to see my smile unfold
He would just wait to see me smile all day then he'd say
That for him only my smile would shine up his whole day

He would smile *His Smile* Back At Me So Sweet
Our eyes would always meet then he would just wink
Back in the days sharing our love as soon as we'd meet
It seems just like yesterday but now he is gone in a blink

His eyes would glance over to find me in such anticipation
My eyes looking back at **His Smile** would I always greet
The twinkle in my eyes that told him I was his all right
His Smile was all that needed to know I was his true date

Still in the days of the present I so quite often repeat
Memories over and over back in the days of our love so sweet
Now I am the one that just sits all alone still waiting
For **His Smile** as my eyes remembering his sweet ways

Now I go back again to **His Smile** tears still in my eyes
I stare deep into the dark long nights I just simply cry
Remembering **"His Smile"** and his love for me all the while
For it was him always just waiting for *me* just to smile

I miss **His Smile** so much as each passing day for me is hell
Just hoping and praying **His Smile** I will again see one day
I know one beautiful day in Heaven we will finally both stay
For our love will shine through the clouds in it's final call

Even though it was he who loved My Smile back then so much
The love I have for him creates the urge to see *His Smile* again
But the one thing I will always miss the most besides his touch
Is the one thing that forever lingers from all of our days of love

Is the only thing that still lingers and distinctly plays in my mind
Even as I remember watching him all of the while all the time
It can be found nowhere for I have searched and it I still can't find
Is *His Wonderful Beautiful Smile*, not mine!

Rose Portillo

I Lied

I Lied To You My Dearest Darling
I'm Sorry When I Said "I Did Not Care"
I Lied Again Dearest "Love Of Mine"
That You Would Be The One In Tears

For It Is I Who Now Sits Alone And Cries
To Be Without You I Simply Cannot Bear
I Still Long For You And Your Loving Arms
Dying Because Your Smile Is No Longer Here

I Lied To You "My Dear Sweetheart"
When I Said We Had So Much More Time
I Lied To My Dearest Baby's Precious Heart
When I Said Without You I Would Be Fine

It Was All Just A Big Lie "My Love"
For Without You Here I Could Never Be Fine
Living Our Lives Together Was What I Prayed
The Crime Committed Was When I Did Not Stay

For Now You Life Is Buried Under The Deep Sod
But Not My Love For You And My Pain, "My God!"
Now "My Love" For The Rest Of My Stricken Life
I Will Forever Be Longing To Be Dying By Your Side

For It Is Not True "My Dear" I Lied When I Would Say
I Did Not Cry I Did Not Hurt That It Was All Okay
Yeah Right The Pain Is What I Know I Now Deserve
This Broken Heart Of Mine Will Never Ever Go Away!

Rose Portillo

Endless Tears

As I still reminisce over our now "Days Of Old"
In my arms the sorrow no one could not have known
I held you beside me as your essence became mine
The memory in my mind will always forever shine

The Countless Tears that now flow from my eyes
I can still visualize your smile as I go back in time
Yesterday is gone though still I will never say goodbye
When I think of tomorrow and all my heartfelt cries

The Endless Tears have filled an ocean by now
Patiently I wait believing you'll come for me somehow
Each breath that I take gives me more pain as I wait
For the promise you gave me not knowing our ill fate

There are Endless Tears I still cry for you even as I pray
Hoping to go home with you "Please don't make me stay!"
Each second I pray to leave for I know you cannot return to me
My aching of this heart I feel destined to be here for all eternity

If only in a dream I could just see your smile once more
Holding me until that sweet day as I wait to end this sorrow born
Waiting still Forever and a Lifetime until the promise is done
Still I cannot believe that your presence from me is truly gone

Still "Endless Tears" in this hell of mine my eyes do not stop
They keep swelling deep inside of my heart until they drop
Endless Tears continue to fall to my aching soul filled to the top
To suffer the guilt I feel for the Endless Time we are apart

Please tell me that they are all wrong and that you are not gone
For it is only you that can truly heal my pain that is all I know
I rather wait with "Endless Tears" and Endless Years all alone
Than to have never loved you or ever held you close to my soul!

Rose Portillo

I Feel You

I Can Actually Feel Your Warm Spirit
As I Move Slowly Throughout My Days
Brushing Right Through Me Even As I Lay

Memories Of A Touch As My Hair You Brush
Lingering Inside My Mind As I Long To Feel
Allowing Me To Reminisce Forever So Much

I Feel You Walking Sometimes Beside Me Too
Haunting Me Any Which Way That You Could
The Soft Heaviness Upon Me Changes My Mood

I Do Not Fear I Know That It Only Feels Like You
It Is My Only Comfort In The Lonely Nights Of Blue
Your Promise You Have Kept For Me Yes It Is True

You Are The Cool Breeze Deep In The Warm Nights
Tasting Your Lips Sweetly Brushes A Kiss On My Face
Letting Me Know You Have Not Left Me That's Right

I Know It Is You I Feel As I Breathe Your Soul In The Air
Tingling Inside Me With Your Lost Felt Love Still There
Feeling Praying Your Presence Is Very Much Still Here

The Days Of Our Lives Everywhere Supposedly Gone
Everyone Telling Me I Must Forget You And Get On
They Don't Know You Live With Me In All Our Songs

Though The Endless Distance Between Us Is So Clear
Why Don't They Know That I Feel You So So Very Near
As I Feel Your Tingling Caress On My Forehead Sincere

And Although They Can Say That We Are Now Apart
I Feel You Your Presence Of Spirit Even So In Your Heart
Now And Forever I Believe As I Take A Breath In Deep

In Your Existence I Breathe You In Our Sweet Love I Keep
No Way Can It Be Anything Other Than You "My Love,"
Even Though How For I Know You're In Heaven Above

Rose

The Pain Found

SO LOST IN THE DEPTHS OF THE REALMS OF NEVER
STOLEN BY THE DEVIL HIMSELF TO REMAIN IN HELL
INCAPABLE OF FEELING ANY LOVE STILL STAYING INSIDE
CAPTURED NOT TO GIVE HOPE OF ANY RELIEF SUBSIDE

ANY PAIN FOUND LYING DEEP WITHIN REMAINS FOREVER
SO MUCH ALIVE TRYING SOLELY TO HURT AND SURVIVE
SITTING WITHIN THE FOLDS OF UNCOVERED PURE LOVE
TRYING TO REACH THE TOP OF SINKING RESIDUALS ABOVE

DAILY ALWAYS PRETENDING TO BE OPENED AND PRIED
DEADLIER THAN ANY SOUL CAN HOPE TO STAY ALIVE
ONLY TO BECOME SECRETLY MORE SECURED IN DECEIT
AS EACH HURT AND PAIN EVENTUALLY IS BURIED TO DIE

ROSE PORTILLO

Death

Death I Ask You Now For What I Saw
Where Is The Soul You Entered Along
I Love Him So But To You He Belongs?

This Intrigues Me It Makes Me Wonder Why
Who You Really Love Has Never Been Told
For Your Soul I Feel . . . Another Form Of Old

Can You Tell Me Death Where Have You Gone?
Tell Me Now Is It Me That You Do Not Love?
Is It Destiny? I Wonder . . . Will I Ever Know

But Tell Me Please Or Death You Forever Go
Now Tell Me What Did You Do With My Love?
Why Did You Take Him Where Is His Soul?

Minu

Amazing Love

Amazing how his love for her still grows
Although now lying underneath the deep sod
Nothing she would do could ever be wrong
He made it all right for to him she belonged

Amazing walls he broke even strong she had built
With the strength of his undying love lies no guilt
He made her whole with her need to be understood
That no one could see through nor that they would . . .

Daring is what was needed of these spirits of two
The very thing he held for her always to stay true
Lacking all that was not done is what they took
Deep inside each other's soul is where they looked

Until this moment now not a day or night goes by
Hearing her prayers to see his smile across the sky
Listening to wind carrying his laughter far away smiles
Where he lies now still her tears falling all the while

Amazing Love strong is the only reason he forgave
Carrying this love inside forever for her to be saved
The tears of sadness of their love existing in her eyes
Tis the reason he is the Angel of Amazing Love up high

Rose Portillo

Badly

Badly I wait patiently for . . . nothing still
For your return to my world now is so unreal
Holding you deep within the depths of my soul
All the memories seeking out will never unfold

I feel I will never be able to again see your face
Though it is when you are near me I feel free
That day the last chance for us to be saved
Again I played the devil's fool as usual to be

They say you can never be again but yes you stay
Although I know I may want to pretend my way
I will forever badly plea "Please Let It Be."
Forever I will always plea Forever and Eternity

I live only for your existence to finally come
I long for the kisses that your lips I want from
Until that day I will wait and I will always long
There is nothing that makes me feel I am wrong

For I know that you are and you will always be
I believe this with all of my heart oh they will see
What you promised to me in the deep dark night
Your spirit has already fulfilled I know this indeed

Minu

I Want To Meet You Death

I Want To Meet You Death In It's Time
My Purpose Is Clear Yet Remains Unsaid

Though The Reasons So Unreal It Seems To Turn
You And I Must Understand What We Will Learn

I Want To Meet You Death Under The Sun
Together Forever We May Simply Run

Now Without Your Existence Making Me See
What I Do Not Understand To Finally Be

Do You Death Also Carry A Burden Unfree?
Will Using My Life Justify Your Needs?

I Want To Meet The One Who Took My Love
I Want To See You Death A Challenge Undone

Is The Underworld Determined Destined By My Soul
When My World Is Tainted With You This I Know

Minu Portillo

A Loving Kiss

When I See A Loving Kiss I Can Remember
How We Were When We Were Once Together
The Air In Which You Once Breathed Along With Me
I Breath In Vain Today Because All I Do Is Grieve

Each Time I Pass By That Lonely Sacred Place
Where I Promised With A Loving Kiss To Be Yours
I Can't Help But Reach Out To Touch You As I Pass
Only To Grasp Emptiness And Air Slapping My Face

I Remember Your Look That You Would Give To Me
That Certain Look Taking Me Back To A Place In Time
Praying And Hoping Today You Could Take Me There
Wishing That Maybe Time Lapse I Can Find You Here

Rose

Broken Dreams

Where did all of our dreams go?
What happened to all our plans?
The happiness that no longer stands
Stolen from us with the force of your hands

Who's anger did you put here anyway?
Who's pain did you hide back in the days?
This chain of abuse from your childhood came
With you inside your sad heart we all paid!

How can you erase the hurt that you caused?
With all the ugly words and forgiveness that is lost
The old days are gone and we have now all paused
With wounds that lie deep within having no cause!

The pain you felt when you were a child
Cannot be rid of and has never been worthwhile
Not only does it spread like cancer it is vile
In return causing so much pain for tomorrow

The never-ending story of torment and abuse
You lie to yourself and just say it was not you
Trying to avoid the world and of being accused
For they might see all my pain and your shame

To have love for someone that hurts us so
Brings sadness all around us even though
You still don't understand why I had to go
Still trying to justify what you have not told

Rose, Abused.

God's Will

When you take something that is wrong in your life,
That will create sorrow you receive only strife.
If there was something that was not meant to be,
Why try to get more than what God wants us to see

The mistakes we make always trying to get more
With no knowledge or concept of the consequences to be
For the consequences will surely be knocking at your door
Unless it is God's Will a price you will pay please believe

Imperfections we allow only making our lives a mess
Instead on God and His loving wisdom we should rely
For God makes no mistakes and causes no stress
For we only hurt ourselves creating all to be tried

Sad that we choose to learn and do things our way
Human nature has shown that we do not seem to learn
Don't we know that God's tears fall each and every day
When we still do not realize that we do not have to burn!

Rose Portillo

Forgive Me Lord

Forgive me, Lord
For wanting more than you sent
Forgive me, Lord
For forgetting it is with you he went

Forgive me, Lord
For trying to change your will
Forgive me, Lord
For not understanding it still

For now I see
This is what you want of me
For now I see
He was here just to show me

Forgive me, Dear Lord
Once more . . .
For I never had anyone more beautiful
In my life before

So Forgive me once again, I plead
For trying to hold on
To the most beautiful love
You have given me from above

Forgive me Dear Lord,
For not accepting what you chose
What was supposed to be
His love you wanted me to hold close

Thank you, Dear Jesus
For sending his love only to me
Even if it was for only a moment
Thank you for allowing it to be

It was through him You taught me indeed
The meaning Of True Love his unselfish shown
No one will know just how his love had grown
Without him I would not have ever believed . . .

Rose Portillo

I've Come

I've Come Into Your World
Did You Know You Needed Me

I've Come Into Your World
God Said It Had To Be

I've Come Into Your World
To Guide And Take Care Of You

I've Come Into Your World
To Show You Love and Be Sweet

I've Come Into Your World
A Promise I Will Keep

So When I Leave Your World
You Will Not Say

That There Was No One
That Loved You This Way

Rose Minu

Man and Woman

Man and Woman
They Search For Forever In Each Other
In Every Corner Of Their Hearts

It Is They That Really Matters The Most
Yet It Is They Our World Has So Little Regard
To Love Is All The More Wonderful In Our Hearts

It Will All End One Day Soon Though
Their Secret With The Unknown Existence
When They Find What They Search For

Then The World Will Come To Finally Know
All That Was Needed For Those Two Beautiful Souls
Is All That Everlasting Evanescent Love Holds

Because Through Every Famine Throughout Eternity
Through Every War There Will Never Not Be
Man And Woman Searching For Their Everlasting Love To Be

Rose

You Are Here

I Feel Something Very Strange Indeed
As I Stand Here Alone Once Again Today
Something Warm Standing Near Me I Perceive
Even In The Unseen It Is Shown So I Believe

In The Darkest Hours Of All While I Lay Awake
I Feel Your Spirit Come For My Soul To Take
I Turn To You Though Thinking You're Still Gone
Because I Only Find Air Between Us And The Wall

Showing My Heartache My Tears Begin To Fall
I Can Hear Your Laughter Now Passing In The Air
I Know Your Spirit Brushes Right Through My Hair
But This Destiny I Realized That I Alone Chose

I Remember Now Your Touch Of Your Love
As Your Spirit Lingers Here Escaping From Me There
Counting The Timeless Days That Have Already Gone
Only Reaching Out To Nothing Crying My Endless Tears

I Remember Your Soft Brown Eyes Looking Into Mine
As I Stare Into The Deep Dark Sky That You Left Behind
Dreading Yet Another Endless Night We've Been Apart
With The Swelling Aching And Deep Pain In My Heart

The Days Of Our Yester Love Keeps Passing On
As I Quietly Feel Your Presence Lingering By My Side
I Breathe You Into My Soul As I Sing Your Loved Song
Assured It Will Be You Again In My Sleep Tonight I Belong

With Every Beating Of My Heart I Will I Must Still Wait
Forever Searching In The Unknown Finding This Ill Fate
Fearing I Will Never Again Find You And Your Sweet Love
Come To Me Tonight For I Know In My Dreams It's Enough

Rose

I Knew You Once

I knew you once a very long time ago
I thought your heart was pure like Gold
You and I were very young then though
There was no corruptness inside your soul

I know you differently now in these days
It seems so very difficult for your heart to stay
It is hard for your heart to be warm again pure
You do not even love me of this I am sure

It is okay Sweetheart you can leave me be
I won't put pressure I won't hold you back
I want someone to love me not make me sad
I cannot hold on your heaviness I cannot bear

I have been good and sweet to your heart
I gave you all my love and you broke it apart
You could not I thought be from up above
For all along it is only me that has felt love

Rose

I Remember

I remember crying so hard at my curse for knowing
For it brought the thought of losing you and our love

I remember I could not cry for being so afraid
I remember knowing the day I lost you I was too late

I remember all your happiness was being with me
It was all I ever wanted for both of us to be

And now as I reminisce and know you lay at rest
I remember all the beautiful times of you and me

I see no happiness here for being without you is the worst
I'm so numb though no longer crying that I won't believe

Then crying so hard not being able to perceive you any longer
I feel no other feeling but being blue from never being free from you

Rose Portillo

I Understand

I understand but I cannot bear the hurt so strong
The aching pain of why my lost love is still gone
The kind of love so dear so sweet only he brought
So long ago that my heart no longer looks above

So broken so torn so sad I keep I cannot sleep
Praying and begging from this world I cannot leave
To go where my loved one is until then will I weep
When he left this earth he took my soul leaving a hole

I understand why my heart is now so awfully cold
Turning inside itself never ever to be shown
Only way I see this through is to get out of this world
Dreading the day I leave for fear I still won't see

Each day is a struggle to escape life's daily pain
Continually seeking day and night for him to come again
To dry the tears from my eyes taking me home with him
But never does this aching song ever leave my heart

I believe I understand now maybe all too well
The urge to leave it all and everything I love behind
To go where no one dares to go this I'll never tell
If I get to my special land maybe him will I find

I understand all too well the crushing stays in my heart
That no one will ever care or want to know my fate
All along wanting to hide my sadness and to intoxicate
I cannot bear not knowing if "My Love" I'll again find

Rose Minu

I Wait Knowingly

Searching With Every Breath I Take
Every Life That Passes Through My Veins
Still I Look For You In Every Crowd I See
I Find You Not You Are No Where To Be

Everyone I See Keeps Walking On By
My Wishes To See Only You With My Eyes
Patiently Praying And Hoping I Always Cry
They All Tell Me Now To Stop No I Will Not

I Wait For Our Memories With You To Return
Tears I Shed Forever Falling Down Being A Fool
They Stain My Face And My Cheeks Yes They Burn
I Know You Are Here Somewhere Even Though . . .

Underneath The Sod Of The Earth You Lay Still

Rose

In All The Vastness

In All The Vastness
Of This Poor Empty Heart

I Search For Your Arms

In The Deep Darkness Of My Life
I Found The Turmoil I Was In

I Search For Your Soul

In The Brightness Of The Morning
In The Laughter Of The Air

I Found Me In Your Heart
Of Your Spirit

Within The Soul Of Your Guiding Love

Rose

It Was You

It Was You Who Had A Part Of My Soul
All This Time You Were There Deep Inside
Together In Some Time Some Place Long Ago
Our Spirits Finding Love Again Very Much Alive

Lost Though In Tomorrow's Hopes And Dreams
Tears Fall When I Think Of Your Eyes So Grim
Eyes Of Truth Though Searching Down Deep Within
Feeling Your Will Reaching For My Heart's Gleams

Hurting Waiting To See What I Needed To Know
Never Did You Know That I Had Never Once Told
You Were Everything That I Was Even I Knew Then
You Come Here Now To Take Me Back Home Again

Only You I Love I've Been Waiting For You Since Then
The Memory Lingers On So You Came Back As I Yearn
Left To The Unknown Never Thinking You Wouldn't Return
Searching For My Love It Was You It Had Always Been

Love, Rose Minu

Lifetime Ago

It began a lifetime ago with you and me,
Tell me though what it was that we were
For I know whatever it was for us we still are
Together we were back again of this I'm sure

With the depths of my heart and my soul,
You came into my life and gave me your heart,
And no one else could try to break us apart
For the spirits do not neglect to tell me so

Queen of Your Heart I am a lifetime ago
The King of My Soul always you are
In this lifetime even as your spirit soars
Queen of Your Heart I still play the part

Let me take a hold of your spirit wings
Take me to the endless winds high in the sky
For I belong to you for this I will Forever sing
The heavens are with you let my love for you fly

Rose Portillo

Meant To Be

Some Say It Was Not Meant To Be
I Tell Myself Then How Could We Be?
You Were Everything That Was In My Life
As I Was There A Part Of Yours

So I Ask Now, "What Part Of Us?"
Do They Claim Was Not Meant To Be
When You Are Still Here For Me
As I Carry You Inside Of My Heart

If We Were Not Meant To Be
Why Did You Enter My World?
You Came Into My Heart Only Once
You Haven't Left Me I Will Not Let You Go

Is It Simply That You Were Not Meant To Stay
If This Is Please Always Remember This . . .
Maybe If You Would Have Stayed Longer
Our Days Together Would Have Turned Sour

Then . . . What Was Meant To Really Be
Is For You To Always Stay
Beautiful In My Heart
And An Angel Like You Are To Me

Rose

Music

Music Brings You Back To Me
It Brings You Closer To My Soul

The Pain And Loneliness You Left
Turns Into Memories Remaining So Sweet

Music To My Ears As You Held Me Tight
Seeps Into My Soul To Some Far Away Place

It Finds Me Locked In Your Kisses So Soft
Takes Me To Heaven Where I Know You Are

Music I Find Now Is My Only Friend Again
It Keeps My Mind From Going Insane

Music Calmly Brings You Back To Me Again
It Keeps Me With You . . . All Through The Night

Music Never Fails To Ease My Aching Heart
It Takes Me Right To You Time And Time Again

It Keeps Me Where I Want To Always Be
Until The Day When You Will Come Back For Me

I Wait For You My Love Meanwhile I Will Stay
With Music That Can Help Take Me Away

Music Is My Only Companion Now With You Gone
In This Lonely World As For You I Still Wait

Minu

My Curse

My curse an illness bringing me excruciating pain
Undoubtly caused by my endless enduring heartache
Obviously trying to reach you even through my death,
I asked for this and pleaded for my cross to bear

My Plea with the pain it brought I feel still today
Tormenting my dreams and torturing my days
The stinging aching pain burning inside my veins
Wanting so dearly for any sin I may have I could pay

Help me Lord Give Me Strength Now I Plead
Pain reams in every breath waiting death I do breathe
This I prayed to be for him I will want forever to see
Even if it takes my curse bringing death for me to be

Because the heartache I hide so well no one knows
Has spread throughout and all inside my bones
Into the stabbing burning pain my sin now shows
Bringing me to my knees only to you Lord I pray

Praying to let me escape the burning flames of life
To reach never ending land of peace with him I stride
Peace from my heartache and suffering more within
Freedom from my curse and my tortured life I live in

Take me now to the land of peace Dear God again I plea
For there seems to be no end to this torturing seed
The end of my unenduring pain I want it to now be
I know it will finally be the day that I see him for real

Rose

The Sad Darkness

Here I Sit In The Room Of The Sad Darkness
For What Seemed Like An Eternity From Hell

On What Seemed The Darkest Night Of All
You Stood In The Dark Crying Out For Me To Tell

You Invited Me To Stay Here With You Forever
Into The Depths Of The Sad Darkness Deep Within

Why Then Do I Still Look For You In The Deep End
Every Moment In The Sad Darkness Of Being There

Then Yes I Find You But You Have Never Grown
Out Of My Heart For You Haven't Left My Soul

Minu

My Destiny

Alas! I Have Found My Destiny

You . . . Were The Joy Of My Life

I . . . Was Always In Your Heart

There Is A Greater Power
Which Enfolds My Every Desire

My Need Is To Exist In Whatever World You Are In
Your Essence Embedded With My Very Soul

A Wish So Very Long Ago . . .
Became My Regret Since Then
I Can Never Be Without

I Will Die Just To See My Desire
I Will Live To Fullfill My Wish
I Will Go Through The Depths Of Fire

Yet Still I Cannot Fullfill All You Require
They Know Not The Wish Of My Heart
My Soul Without Your Essence Cannot Depart . . .

For I Was Created Always
To Be With You Forever . . .

To Be . . . My Destiny . . . You Are

Rose Portillo

My Love,

My Beautiful Love;

It Was Always Only You In My Eyes,
No Other Person Could I See,
No Other Thing Did I Ever Need

Your Beautiful Heart Was Al ways Within

My Love I Had For You Was Genuine
Life Now Is So Sad For You Left Me Much Too Soon

All That I Lived For Fell To Ruin
To The Ground It Went Right Through
For What Instigated Life's Anger And Doubts

Life Today For Me Is Not Worth Living In
And Cannot Be Lived In If It Is You Lived Without

And Now Here Stands All That Is False . . .
And All That Remains Is Nothing . . .
For Everything That Was Real Is Gone

When I Lost You I Lost Myself
All That Was Right Became Wrong,

My Love,

My Beautiful Love.

Rose

My Love God Sent

Reality Hitting Me Way Deep Down Inside
Seeing You Was Heaven's Dream Come True
But Instead Of Joy Only Tears Filled My Eyes
For The Love God Sent Slipped Away Too Soon

My Conscience Having To Deal With God I Cried
Of Vows Spoken Of Love Before You Ever Arrived
Promises To Cherish Forever Only Causing Me Strife
For My Love God Sent Was You Entering My Life

My Honor At Stake With The Heavens Causing Pain
All I Had Been Waiting For Was You To Come Again
Everything You Are Is What I Ever Wanted In A Man
How God Knew What Love To Send Was His Plan

All I Have Done Is Hurt The One I Love The Most
When The Lord Sent You There Was No Other Choice
My Disgrace Is A Broken Promise To The One I Love
Now The Loss Of My Soul's Desire I Must Sacrifice Of

Broken Between Two Kinds Of Love All Of My Life
I Have No Hate I Cannot Hurt For What I Have Saved
Only Hurting Myself Deep Inside Paying My Own Price
Which Is The Way For Both Loves That Want To Stay

If I Leave I Cause Severe Pain For What To Whom?
If I Stay I Will Never Feel My Heart Aglow Within
Torn In Torment Not Trying To Hurt Anyone Again
Sure The One Being Hurt In Reality Is I'm The One

Tell Me Sweet Angel Of Mine That I Think You Are
Someone Must I Hurt For Either Way I Must Part
Who Is It That You Love Are You Doing What Is True
Oh God! My Love You Sent Is It Not For My Heart?

What Are Vows Today If They Only Get Broken Tomorrow
Do I Stay And Wait For My Love Whose No More To Come
Is There Forever In My Misery With All That Pass Me By
Maybe I'll Leave Only To Pay With More Unforgiven Sorrow

Rose Minu

My Soul

I Know You Did Not Do As They Say
You Would Never Hurt Me That Way

The Day They Told Me You Were Gone
My Soul Just Froze My Spirit Went Cold

It Was Not True This Pain In My Heart
Now Is A Hole From Emptiness When You Left

I Pretended So Well Yes Of Course I Lived On
This I Knew I Must Do For The Children I Bore

You Took My Spirit Though Of All Joy And Love
The Day You Left You Left Me Without A Goodbye

And I Did Not Know My Soul Was Locked In
It Went With You In The Realm You Have Been

How Could It Be That With Your Soul Mine Is Gone
When As A Thief My Spirit You Just Took It Along

This Must Be A Dream A Lost Dream It Has To Be
Only To Always Awaken To Find You Are Truly Gone

I Need To Find You For Only You Have My Soul
I Did Not Know That It Was You That Chose To Go

Tell Me Please Where You Are Where Did You Go
So That I Can Also Find You My Love And My Soul

Rose

My Tear Stained Pain

My Heart Holds Tired Sounds,
Sounds Of Many Times Of Pain

Of The Love I Have Ever Felt In My Heart,
Is The Only Love That Really Loves To Hurt

The Years Of My Early Happiness Were Stolen
From Beneath The Protection Of My Tear Stained Pain

As Time Grew Old And Memories Lingered On,
No Reassurance Or Comforting Was Allowed Upon

The Memories Hardening With Tear Stained Feelings,
Which Grew Over Protecting The Pain That Lay Hidden

Soon Pain Grew Over Pain Though Covering Only More Pain,
And Tears Falling That Lingered Forever Only Hardening More

And Now As Pain And Tear Stained Hurtful Sad Memories,
Keeping Layers Upon Hardened Hidden Underneath Being

The Smile Of My Heart Can Only Cry Smiling Stained Tears,
Which Make No Sound Which Lay Hidden Secrets Unseen

The Memories Are Unchanged Only Burdened Deeper More,
With Every Second Continually Bringing Blankets Of Warmth

Only To Protect To Protect And Cover My Hardened Heart
Trying To Keep My Tear Stained Pain Forever Hidden Apart

Rose Portillo

My Universe

And You, My Dear
Are My Universe

I Am The Moon
You Are The Sun

I Am Venus
You Are My Lover Moon
Where Only You Belong

I Am The Darkness
You Are The Stars
That Brighten My Night, My Heart

Rose Minu

Only In My Dreams

I CAN STILL FEEL YOUR SOFT WARM BREATH
THOUGH I WALK ALONE YOU I CANNOT SEE,
I KNOW YOUR WARM BODY IS CLOSE TO MINE,
BUT I AWAKE IT'S ONLY A DREAM I THEN FIND

IN THE DEEPEST DARKEST HOURS OF THE NIGHT,
YOUR STILL LIKE PRESENCE DOES COMFORT MY HEART,
AS I DRIFT BACK IN MY MEMORY TO FEEL YOUR ARMS,
REACHING OUT FOR YOUR TOUCH HOW LIFE IS SO UNKIND

HEARING YOUR LAUGHTER AS I HEAR THE BIRDS SING,
YOUR SPIRIT PLAYING ALONG WITH THE WIND SO SWEET,
RUSH DOWN WHERE YOU LIVE DEEP IN MY SOUL I BELIEVE,
THROUGH MY TEARS I CRY I LISTEN TO YOUR BREATHING

AND NOW I CLOSE MY EYES AS I LAY MYSELF TO SLEEP,
I STILL KNOW YOUR LOVE SO CLOSE YOUR DEEP TOUCH,
WISHING I COULD VISIT YOU SOMEWHERE IN MY DREAMS
SO I COUNT THE ENDLESS DISTANCE THAT LIES BETWEEN US.

I SEE YOUR EYES WITH SO MUCH LOVE STARING INTO MINE,
AS BRIGHT AS THE STARS SHINING IN MY DARKEST NIGHT,
WITH TEARS IN MY EYES AND THIS PAIN LYING IN MY HEART,
I HOLD YOUR BEAUTIFUL FACE IN THE PALM OF MY HANDS!

WHILE THE LOVING DAYS OF OUR YESTER YEARS PASS ON,
AS I STAND HERE FEELING YOUR SPIRIT WITH ME ALL ALONG
THEN I BREATHE YOU IN AGAIN RIGHT BACK INTO MY SOUL,
I KNOW YOU ARE HERE WITH ME YOU WILL NEVER BE GONE

I CONTINUE TO SEARCH WITH EVERY BEAT OF MY HEART,
ONLY TO LAY AWAKE WAITING FOR YOU NIGHT AFTER NIGHT,
YOU NEVER LEAVE MY MIND FOR YOU DROWN IN MY TEARS
BUT NOW I KNOW YOU WILL FOREVER BE ONLY IN MY DREAMS!

ROSE PORTILLO

I See Her

I KNOW SHE'S IN A LOT OF PAIN
BUT I SEE HER AND MY HEART BREAKS

I'M IN THE MIDDLE OF IT ALL
IT HURTS ME TO SAY

I RATHER BE WITH HER
THAN ANYONE ELSE IN THE WORLD

IF I COULD I WOULD HELP HER
BUT IT SEEMS TO HER I JUST DON'T

I DON'T KNOW HOW TO
BUT I AM FOR HER I LOVE HER

NESSIE; MY GRANDDAUGHTER

Our Story

God Knew . . .

Our Love Began When We Were Very Young,
We Did Not Know His Angels Had Already Sung
God Knew That When We Met,
That Even With Time We Would Never Forget

God Also Knew That In Time We Would Find,
We Could Not See What He Had In Mind

God Saw Our Future Before We Even Knew,
That From Our Lives What We Needed To Pursue

The Sufferings And Lessons We Needed To Learn,
To Have More Patience And Find Love In Return

So When We Came To Meet Once Again,
We Would Appreciate Our Love Heaven Sent

Rose Marie Minu Portillo

Our Story So Long Ago

So Long Ago When First We Met
Somehow I Know Though We Knew
We Would Be Together And Never Lose
On Our Hearts So Long Ago Were Set

No Matter How The World Had Tried
We Never Allowed Not A Single Soul Inside
As Even Once More Again Even Spirits Hold
As Sure As Our Tears We've Shed And Cried

Time And Time Again We Were Torn Apart
From Their Evil Doings Until The Day We Died
Spirits Strong In Love Eachother Again We Find
Our Love Forever Goes On Strong In Our Hearts

So This Is Our Story Of Love Not So Long Ago
The Great Story Of A Stolen Forbidden True Love
A Love So Great Yet So Strong Having To Be Told
All The World Knows Our Story So Very Long Ago

Rose Portillo

Please Don't Ever Leave!

You Held Me Close To Your Heart Once
As I Cried In My Fears Afraid To Be Alone
Wanting Then So Crazy Desperately Not To Die
Only In Your Arms To Stay By Your Side

"Please Don't Ever Leave Me," I Pleaded In Tears
I Don't Want To Live Without You Always Stay Near
So You Promised Me That You Would Never Go
But Then Spirits Took You Away From My World!

Why? Why Would They Do This, I Ask Thee?
Why? Why Couldn't They Leave You Here With Me?
If I Have To Die Without You It's Being Said
I Will Die Looking To Always Find You Again

Don't They Know I Cannot Exist,
Without The Other Part Of My Soul?
Tell Me Where You Are So I Must Go
Tell Them Your Essence Is My Every Existence!

You Are What I Live For Even In The Past
Tell Them To Bring You Home Give Me One More Chance!
So I Can Give You My Love That Lives Inside
This Love This Heart That Just Will Not Die!

You Were Torn Right Out Of My Life!
Just Like The Terrors Of My Forever Fears Arrive
They Don't Care Here To Bleed My Heart Lies
I Still Believe To Find And See You Alive!

Just To See You Believing That You Are Here
But I Search Everywhere No Matter What I Do
Still Asking To Where Did Your Essence Leave To?
Tell Me Where Did The Other Half Of Me Go?

I Pretend No More Or Forget Don't They Know?
I Am Lost In A Dream Always Searching The Unknown
So Lost Inside A Sad Lonely Dream, God! So Unkind
Wandering The Dark Cold Empty Streets All Alone

Waiting For You To Come And Take Me Home
Tell Me This Is Reality You Are Here And What I Feel
Lingering Over Me It Is You Not Leaving Me Still
Show Me While I Cry Erase All My Tears I Shed

Your Gentle Spirit Tries To Take My Fears Away
Have You Come Back To Me Already Somehow?
Yes Since Then You Know That I Needed You So!
It's The Reason You Promised To Never Let Me Go!

Rose Portillo

You are My World, My Love My Life.

What would have happened
Had you never looked for me that one night?
Had we never saw each other that one day?
What would I be doing sitting here alone
Without you in my life now?

For because of the death of my friend
It was you that my life had began

When I think of this I know . . .
With you here it is to be by my side

I would be very sad and so all alone though
It's so sad that it had to be this way
But I am very happy that your life came my way

I don't know why we met
But I know God knows for sure
Someone once reminded me
That God doesn't make mistakes . . .

So therefore our destiny was to find each other
To love each other and be good to each other . . .

Thank God we saw each other that day

You are My World.
You are My Love.
You are My Life.

I Love You

Pa Mi Querida

Reincarnation

I Loved You So Long Ago Quietly Knowingly,
I Never Failed You Though I Always Failed You

Your Words Were Always Songs Of Joy To Me,
They Reached Out And Showed Your Love Inside

Your Lips Were Warm And Forever So Tender,
They Felt The Way I Once Knew Them To Be

Your Life Was Needed In Someone Else Though,
For Your Love Could Not Be Fullfilled This Way

Someone Other Than You Beautifully Understood,
To Be Able To Love Me Needing Your Soul To Stay

For Without The Pain It Caused We Could Not,
You Sent Your Love To Me Still Here I Knew

Your Life I Know Someone New Brings Your Love,
Tender Again But Your Lips I Feel Anew

Though They Are As They Were Back Then,
Your Heart, I Feel It And I Know For Real

I Feel Your Sweet Beautiful Love With Me,
Your Heart And Your Soul . . . Like When

Are Here With Me Once Again.

Rose Minu

Someone Like You

Even Because Of Someone Like You
It Will Never Be The Way It Used To Be

There'd Be No Shine In His Eyes Like Yours
His Smile Would Not Be The Same

Looking In His Eyes I Would Know
That You Are Still No Where To Be Found

Searching For That Same Kiss From Him
Would Be Similar But Certainly Not The Same

I Would Know Deep Inside Of My Heart
He May Be Someone Like You

But There Could Never Ever Be Anyone Like You
No . . . Not The Sweet You That You Were To Me

Rose

Sometimes, Dear Lord

Sometimes, Dear Lord
I Wish You Would Send The Rain
To Wash Away The Tears And My Pain

Sometimes, Dear Lord
I Pray You Send Me All Your Love
With The Touch Of An Angel From Above

Sometimes, Dear Lord
At Night I Cry For Your Comfort
Like A Blanket Of Warmth On My Heart

Sometimes, Dear Lord
I Sing For Your Mercy And Your Grace
May You Rush It Please To My Place

Sometimes, Dear Lord
I Sigh Knowing You Will Come
To Send For Me Finally To Go Home

Sometimes, Dear Lord
I Dream Of Your Promise
To Cleanse All The Strife Among Us

Make It All Go Away, Dear Lord . . . I Pray, I Beg
Sometimes, Dear Lord.

Rose Portillo

Still

It Was I Who Failed To Believe
It Was I Who Really Believed . . .
You Were Always There Then And Again
You Are Here Somewhere In My Dreams

I Cried Then Wanting You So Badly
I Cry Now Still Wanting You So Sadly
You Haunt My Days With All The Memories
Lingering In My Nights Painfully Lovingly

Wishing I Could Reach Out And Touch You
Your Haunting Presence Is Ever In My Arms
Not You Nor Anyone Will Or Could Ever Undo
What My Heart Cries To Touch Still Ever Apart

I Know You Tried So Hard For Me To Stay
Your Spirit's Lingering Forever Too Though
I Truly Have You Here But Why Is It So Cold?
Unfrightened Will I Forever Reach For Your Caress

I Wait For Your Soul To Walk With Me In The Dark
For The Day That Comes As I Die We Will Meet Again
Your Undying Spirit I Know Without Me Will Never Rest
Until You Are One With My Very Own Soul Forever In

Rose Minu

Struggle Of Love

It Can Be Frightening To Find True Love
To Feel The Heartache True Love Can Bring
So Heavy Deep Within So Unbearable To Live With
The Struggle Of Love A True Love Which Can Be

So Many Times In The Years Of Yesterday
Gone Only To Be The Emptiness Of Tomorrow
His Juliet Who Continued To Forever Search
For Her Romeo Lost Together Only In Death

The Strong Envious Force Of Love's Destiny
Sadly Imprisoned By A Love We Cannot Have
With True Love's Hope Done Always Ever Before
No Meaning To Forever Just Being Together

Struggling If Once Our Love Is Finally Found
Cruelness Seems To Enter Only For To Destroy
We Never Leave To Feel Any True Love At All
Only To Return And Continue To Search For Love

For You . . . For Me . . . For The Struggle Of Love

Minu

Sweet Dreams

Wishing I'm not living in loneliness for most of my life
Always forever dreaming and praying in hopes of despair
Crying with tears trying to see your face just one more time
Being all I wished for but now only in my sweet dreams

But if I must ever leave this ugly cruel world that I am in here
I won't ever have any of my dreams while I cry and mourn
So even if I take my life and if I should die it's you I won't see
It is inevitable I will always try to see your face in sweet dreams

But then why does it seem I still cannot find you in my dreams
Maybe I will no longer be able to dream of you being by my side
All I know is it hurts that no longer can I ever see your beautiful face
Except maybe only if I am able to find you in my sweet dreams

So I pray to God to allow me to keep living just a little longer
So maybe I will be able to keep dreaming of you aching in pain
Praying I live to keep trying to find you somewhere in my dreams
But maybe if I can pretend you are here while I call your name

I pray to my Almighty God who makes my miracles come true
That I will always have my sweet dreams allow me to see you
I see your beautiful face and feel your love so I'll be yours again
Sweet dreams are the only way I can actually be with you forever

If only I can find you somewhere in my sweet dreams while knowing
This is the only way you will be with me to live with me always
You will be with me whenever I dream of you which is all I have
Sweet Dreams are the only place I always find my way back to you

I will always cherish the moments you gave me forever "My Love"
So to know I can have you whenever so true although you're above
For this is what I want to forever be beside You "Sweet One So Dear"
Though I'm Still Here Alone Dreaming Sweet Dreams Of You Forever

Rose Portillo

The Echoes Of His Sin

The echoes of his unforgiving sins,
Reminding me of all my painful grins
Why does he seek to hurt my heart,
To destroy all my Love and Faith all apart

I think he knows exactly just what he will be
The next victim and his next prey I know we'll see
He pretends to not know just what he has done
With the loving trust that I gave him once

He will forever reach out and always try to find
Just to make his pattern work in due time
The sins of his father sunk deep into his mind
Down the ancient lines of sins still lurking behind

Still in a dark stillness he does still search
For the most naïve and good ones that will believe
And just when he knows he has their hearts to steal
It will be much too late for them to even feel

Then you will hear their cries all those nights
For the Lord God they pray for him to see their tears
As forever suffering still echoes in my heart with strife
For his sins that forever echoe with all these years

Abused Wife
Rose

The Hurt She Gave

The Pain She Gave That Is Still Inside Of Your Heart
And Me Thinking You Would Simply Overcome

Believing I Became The Special Someone In Your Life
You Said It Was I All Your Life You Were Searching For?

But You Still Hide Your Deep Cuts And Wounds Inside
Cuts That You Haven't Really Ever Healed From

Only Covering Your Pain With No Sort Of Ointment
Because The Cut Was Too Deep So How Could It Heal?

So I Thought I Was The One That Was Right For You
Yes But Now I Am The One Paying For The Pain You Feel

For Until You Want To Heal From Your Cuts Deep Inside
I Cannot Take Away The Hurt She Gave That Is So Very Real

Your Damaged And Hurt Heart She Gave Will Never Be Okay
But When You Really Look Deep Inside Of Your Lonely Soul

Really Look Inside To Notice Your Heart Is With Blood Tainting
For The Scars And Pieces Of Your Heart Are Here Left Remaining

Rose Portillo

The Memory

The Truth Revealed At Last
The Memory Of You Returned
Why Certain Memories Chosen
To Be Buried Within Me Burns

You Left Me All Alone And Cold
With Loved Ones That Are Still Here
Knowing They Needed Me In Their Life
Dying For You They Would Be All Alone

If Only My Buried Treasured Memories
Would Have Been Unfolded In My Soul
For I Yearn To Go Where You Go
Disregarding All That Is In This Ugly World

So Had Your Beautiful Haunting Soul
Not Staying Hidden From Me Til Now
Loved Ones Here Would Not Have Grown
To Be The Beautiful Ones With Stories Told

All I Knew Was That It Had To Be
That Your Soul Meet Mine To See
The Depths Of Never Until Eternity
Only You I Will Live For My Memory

Rose Portillo

The Pain Of Our Hearts

The moment I saw your face I knew
The moment you looked in my eyes you too
I knew you were mine from so long ago
I knew you would be mine once again so true

Our hearts were made in the Twilight of The Dawn
They were created from eachother's spirits in a song
Your heart beats with the breath of my soul within
And so the beginning of the story is told and then . . .

How could you possibly know all the unknown
For you exist just to live in the air I now breath
Love occurred the second you looked into my heart
Taking Love's truth from my eyes right into my soul

Is there no end to this heart's pain you forever send
Knowing your spirit is empty not being with mine again
Until your whole life once more will unite with my time
This great love is not hidden not even from the blind

Deep down inside of me you will always stay
We cannot hide Our Precious Love no more no way
You are even felt by them for your spirit lingers in the air
For I breathe your very essence as I wait patiently here

As I continue to walk this earth I can feel the sweet pain
All along I know The Heavens with you soaring above contain
My spirit will always feel all that we grew to know though
That the Pain of Our Hearts is because of Our Sweet Love

So Forever and Eternity with each breath that I take you told
I am empty waiting for the other half of my heart to stop this pain
As I continue to reach out for you and only air my hand grasps
Because I die each second more knowing this as my heart breaks

ROSE MINU

The Promise

The Great Promise That He Made
In The Still Of The Night Held His Soul
Forever More To Me Even In His Grave

Many Years Have Passed And Long Been Gone
All That Was Promised Is Yet To Be Done
His Spirit Undying With All His Will And Might

Yes Each Night Her Tears Still Forever Fall
Down Along Her Face Still For Their Love
His Death Will Never Be Real Ever At All

They Say Many Lifetimes Even As Yet Before
Their Same Felt Love Was So Much More
Still Spirits Holding The Promise Needs To Unfold

So Where He Went Do All Spirits Unrested Go?
They All Live What Is To Us Within The Unknown
But His Undying Promise Is What Still Flows

How Hard For Him But He Needs To Still Keep
From Where Most Spirits Wait And Do Not Sleep
For His Promise For Her Will Forever Still Hold

She Was His Everything In This World And Much More
The Promise He Made Awaits Until She Comes Home
So Of Course He Too Has To Wait For Heaven's Door

Rose Portillo

The Strange Feeling

I've known you from somewhere before
The sight of you was forever so bold
Oh and I've loved you even if so forlorn
Envisioning our souls will forever soar

I've felt your kiss so real still loved evermore
The moment our lips met our souls again lived
I knew you were mine always even then
So many lifetimes ago and many years before

When I first made love to you it stayed
My heart belonged to you becoming so true
You were in my soul everyone else knew
You said I was in your blood yes for me too

Our kisses were of old though I know you know
Like the deepened folds of a soft petalled Rose
Still ever deep within our spirits as our lives told
Enriched forever and ever softly dwell in our souls

Every thought of you I am there somewhere still
How can this destiny of us that was not be real
With your love and your forever touch so close
Every heartbeat I felt against my chest I still feel

Who are you My Love but where did you go?
You know me do you not but why are you gone?
Who am I still and who are you too with me?
Without you I am nothing for you I was born to see

Rose Portillo

The Sunset I See

The Sunset I See Is The One Thing
Brings Your Smile Back To Me

The Roaring Waves Come Crashing In
Brings Your Laughter To My Ears Within

The Warmth Of The Morning Sun Against My Skin
Bring The Softness Of Your Body Next To Mine

Everywhere I go Everything I do
You Are There I Cannot Undo
This Untouched Unfailing Love I Have For You

As I Close My Eyes In The Night So Deep
With Hopes Of A New Day Dawn Yet Not One

Bringing Your Love So Sweet So United Done
Back To My Memory Because You're Still Gone

Rose Portillo

I Ask You

Why did you leave me here all alone,
In this cruel ugly world only to be stoned?
Without your smile, tender arms and loving touch,
They hate me so I can't help but cry up above.

I still feel your warmth beside me though,
The peace it gives bringing your touch so soft.
Praying once again for your face I could see,
Just like back then all the while we were in glee.

People always tell me how I must let you go,
They seem to think that I need to be happy now.
Even sad I rather keep holding on don't they know,
To every part that belonged to our every loving vow.

Even though I am left here on earth in dread,
The memory of our love I rather keep than let go.
For to be gone completely I will lose control of it all,
So I pretend I wait for you telling the world instead.

Though no one really cares and it doesn't matter none,
What I feel they can never know so why should I care?
And the years have brought nothing but sadness along,
My heart is dying and his soul carries my death in it's toll.

So I ask you in search of you will I forever roam,
Will the spark of our spirits ignite my path to your heart?
Do I still wait for you to come knocking at my door,
To take me home with you where ever you are?

Rose Portillo

You Were The Sunshine

You Were The Sunshine Of My Days
That I Did Not Appreciate

You Were The Songs Of The Birds
That I Could No Longer Hear

You Were My Rainbow In My Sky
But I Always Seemed To Be Blind

You Were The Flowers In The Spring
That I Chose Not To Smell In The Breeze

And Only Now That You Are Gone
I Can Feel Everything You Were To Me

You Are Everything Of What I Have Longed
This Is For All Of Your Heart From All Of My Heart

Rose

You Convinced Me

YOU CONVINCED ME TRULY FINALLY
WHAT WE BOTH ALREADY HAD KNOWN

THAT OUR LOVE WE HAD FOR EACHOTHER
WAS BETTER PUT ON A BOOKSHELF THAN HELD

WAITING PRETENDING THAT THINGS ARE FINE
I'VE ALWAYS WAITED YEARS LEFT BEHIND

THIS WAY IF WE LEAVE THERE'S NO DOUBT
I WON'T FEEL GUILTY ONCE I KNOW I'VE TRIED

TO KNOW WHEN YOU TELL ME IT'S REALLY OVER
AS MUCH AS THE PAIN HURTS THIS I WILL KNOW

NO ONE CAN SAY I DIDN'T DO ENOUGH FOR YOU THOUGH
I'M ALREADY CONVINCED YES YOU WANT IT TOO

GOODBYES ARE ALWAYS HARD ON THE HEART IT'S TRUE
SO I ALWAYS WAIT UNTIL IT'S DONE FOR GOOD

ROSE PORTILLO

Such Evil

There is a horrible and evil generation of people
It's not astonishing how such ugliness even exists
They care less about morals, feelings, hurts or True Love
Not bothering their consciences or affecting their hearts

Outnumbering Good people here on earth it's not shocking
Why these evil people exist and how anyone cannot see
Of course it is that most of the evil is of each other therefore
All are in it together devastating outnumbering the noble

There is of such great nature and rarity to be sweet and kind
Patience is no longer seen or given with gentleness as a virtue
There is a sadness among those whose qualities are of Good
Devastating to the heart of those who always love and forgive

So much tragic devastating that Good People cannot even be near
But it is true only Loving Goodhearted can conquer the hatred
It hurts that so often most just go along with evilness so easily
For the giving from one's heart is a beauty not easily possessed

The Goodhearted Man cannot be conceived or perceived there of
Such great evil that is within a soul and why does it win over
Ugliness is so bad the Good do not want to be within it's reach
For it actually hurts to deal with this evil so Let God and Believe

It has been known that demons go straight for the Kindhearted
It is easy to hurt the Good for rare are the Kind who have no clue
The beautiful do not understand but always forgive that is all they do
For it is their nature to love but it is feared how much evil is alive

Rose Portillo

He Hurt Me

He Hurt Me So Bad I Feel So Used
He Left Me Alone All The Time As I Trace

He Would Say Such Bad Things About Me
And Then He Would Laugh At Me To My Face

I Feel Like An Idiot For He Did It Right Away
Still Feeling Stupid For Not Being Able To See

When He Told Me With A Smile He Loved Her
I Wonder Why By His Side Did I Even Stay

I Was So Kind Trying Hard For Him To See My Love
How Could I Stay While He Kept Saying Goodbye

He Would Hit Me He Would Spit At Me Tell Me Lies
That Is So Much Hate And I Still Don't Know Why

Rose Portillo

What Do You Do?

What do you do when the one you love,
Tells you he doesn't love you anymore?

Do you stop thinking of him or her?
Do you hate them when you still love them?

The only time someone can stop loving you,
Is when they never really ever loved you at all

Please tell my heart to stop hurting stop loving him
Can you help me stop my mind from thinking of him?

How can one stop the aching of the heart now?
Maybe if you say to yourself they never loved you

Please God don't let him hurt my heart anymore
Throw this aching pain away help me let him go

He fooled me so good he knew exactly what to do
It hurts to be treated the way he has treated me

It's okay I know he never loved me for love is not bad
There was only one person that loved me for real

He had my heart in the palm of my hands long ago
He held the key to my heart when no one else could

Tell me what to do now that I know I'm despised
How do I tell myself to let go of the years and all the lies

Rose Portillo

I Miss Him

TO ME HE WAS THE MOST BEAUTIFUL MAN I'VE EVER SEEN
STAYING IN MY HEART HIS BEAUTY I HAVE EVER LAID EYES ON

HE WAS SO SINCERE AS HE NODDED ALWAYS SHOWING MY WAY
AS WE PASSED HE KINDLY SHOWED ME LOVE EVEN IN THOSE DAYS

HIS EYES SAID IT ALL AND HIS LOVING HEART WAS ALL I EVER SAW
I DON'T KNOW WHY BUT THERE WAS A SECRET LOVING JUST FOR
ME

EVERYTIME I WOULD WALK ON BY HIM OUR SECRET WE DID
KNOW
HE GAVE TO ME HE PUT UPON MY SAD FACE HIS BEAUTIFUL SMILE

FOR AS IMPOSSIBLE AS OUR LOVE SEEMED SO BAD WAS MY LIFE
UNTIL THE BEAUTY OF HIS SPIRIT FOR ME ALWAYS SOFTLY SIGHED

IN VIEW OF HIS SMILES I COULDN'T HIDE MY LOVE EVEN IF I
TRIED
GOD I MISS HIM EACH MOMENT STILL TO THIS DAY AS I STAY
ALIVE

I MISS HIS LOVING HEART HE GAVE I MISS HIS SMILE AND HIS
SOUL
HE MADE ME FEEL SO LOVED WITH JUST ONE GLANCE HEAVEN'S
SMILE

REASSURANCE OF WISDOM IS INSIDE OF WHAT I KNOW HE KNEW
HE PUT ME INSIDE HEAVEN'S DOOR I WISH WITH HIM I COULD
GO

ROSE PORTILLO

I Asked The Lord Why

I thanked the day you entered my life
But, I asked the Lord why?

Why, did he have to leave Dear God?
Why, did he have to go?

I asked the Lord why . . .
Why was the world I live in so cruel?
When he left he took my soul with him too.

Again, I asked the Lord why . . .
How could I survive all alone without him?
When he took my whole heart with him he went with you?

How does my heart keep beating,
I ask you Dear Lord,
When with every breath I take it still hurts me so?

Then finally, I asked Dear God can't you see,
He was all that was right in my life,
Our love was not wrong so why should it be.

I asked the Lord why?
I continue to love him so,
For he is my life the other part of my soul.

Then God answered me with signs from above,
Although I know he is gone now,
I can still feel his love
So am I really alone?

I can still see his eyes so sweet
In all of my dreams I can feel your lips so close
With each sigh and every heartbeat.

So I ask The Lord Why,
How can he still be can this be wrong?
That I keep him in my heart all the day long.

So I keep wishing and hoping to soon see the day
When I will feel your spirit come home to stay

Your Rose

Wandering That Way

What happened? Did you ask yourself?
Just a moment ago everyone was here
They were all happy for they loved you
They cheered you on you were the one

It was good you had found your beauty
Where did she go to? What did you do?
Did you say something wrong but no
You couldn't have done that no not you

You were the one with it all and then some
You were the man that held your head high
Everyone envied you when you had her
What happened to you? Your life? Your wife?

Why in just a blink of an eye she was gone
Did you tell her to leave? Did you hurt her?
But wasn't it that you had it all back then?
She had to be the one that made it go wrong

Of course it was her she was no good
That will sound right that will make it allright
Say she was bad all along don't let no one know
It was you that was the one for loss of her hold

You wanted to be the one that had her though
You wanted to be with the others in your life right
How could you do both and still make her happy
You couldn't so one of them had to be the one to go

Well it couldn't be the others oh no not them
If you say that she is no good and she leaves
It will be okay no one will know it was you that erred
So that is what you will say things will look sweet

But why are you sitting on that curb that you are on
What's wrong? Are you sad? Does your heart hurt?
She hurt you? Just finally come to grips with the truth?
It was you that hurt her remember you always left her alone

Yes because I saw her crying all the time in your home
Every time I would stop by I wanted to see you both
She would be waiting for you and yes wondering why
You were always leaving her alone though you were gone

It's okay don't worry cause I saw her yesterday
Yeah she seems to be moving on without you now
She says you wanted it that way you said you'd be okay
But isn't that you each morning wandering that way?

Rose Portillo

But Only For A Moment

To carry my cross this I know
God showed me how this must be so
I realize it was He that sent you now
But only for a moment just to show . . .

To show me your Beautiful Love though
Now you belong to the Lord Above
But only for a moment he allows you to come
Through those times I learned your love

When you spread your wings to fly
How I wish I was the one that died
Though I confess I still don't know why
I feel you still watch me from up high

So but only for a moment with this journey
To be without your smile though I rather die
This is something I will never be able to bear
For I feel your spirit staying with me still here

I carry you on each breath I take as I still ache
Just to see your smile my heart forever breaks
Wishing I'd go in the heavens where you guide
Telling me you are forever here by my side

It is no one else besides you My Angel
But if only for a moment just to feel your touch
As you wipe my tears with your kiss I must cry
I die with all of my love so on your love I rely

*****

Rose

No More Angel

How Could My Angel
Not Be My Angel Anymore?

How Could My Love
Not Be So In Love Like Before?

Tell Me Is This True?
Tell Me Has It All Been A Lie?

Why Would They Say That About You?
Though I Gave You The Alibi

How Could My Angel Not Be
How Can You Not Shine In My Heart?

All The Tears I Shed While You Are Free
I Can't Get Over You All The While Still Apart

Angel Of Mine Are You No More Angel?
They Tell Me You Were Always Just A Guy

It Must Have Been An Illusion Then
For Me To Think Of You So High

Dear Angel Please Tell Me Again
Why Does It Feel Now As If It All Was Just A Sin

Rose Portillo

One Man's Joy

One Man's Joy May Be Another Man's Sorrow
One Man Is Laughing While Another Man Crying
Loving One Woman Both Willing To Die For
Realize Only One Can Be True For The Other A Fool

As The Man With The Woman In His Arms Shows
So Boastful He Has It All Yet So Unappreciatively Told
Thinking As He Fills The Heads Of Others Being So Untrue
What Does One Feel As He Hurtfully Puts Her So Down

One Man Who Truly Loves Her Deep Down Inside His Soul
Hiding All Of His Heart For The Happiness Of Her Life
What Does One Do When He That Has Her Hurts Her So
When The Other Knows He Loves Her Ever So Much More

Does The One Man Who Loves Her So Keep Quietly Unsaid
While The Other Continuing To Hurt Her So Deeply Foiled
One Man Laughs While The Other Will Keep And Love Her
He Smiles But Karma Has It She Will Be Loved By The Other

Rose Portillo

Destiny Of Fates

As she entered my soul with just one glance
Her beauty enchanted completely unmatched
I unresistingly gave in to her loving substance
As she whirled me around I was lost in her trance

Looking deeply in her beautiful hypnotizing eyes
Across her bed upon her reddish brown hair I lie
As she held me so tight so very near to her heart
I swore to my death with her I would never depart

All of this I know it would never be over for me
Forever to stay together was Our Destiny of Fates
I swore to her I would find her wherever anywhere
So true she was already inside my my soul in my heart

Although she could not be found the day that I died
Her precious soul I had entered like magic as she cried
Where did she go though when she left me and why?
For her tears for me she will forever endlessly still cry

I sent them to look for her she was no where to be found
I will find her anywhere I swore in life wherever she may go
You will see even after my death Her I will find this I vowed
For my soul will be with her then as it is still now I said so

When she pleaded with me with all her heart that last night
To never let her go never leave her alone or from my sight
My vow I gave her in heart with a very beautiful loving kiss
Even in my death you will know it is her I will always miss

It's been so many years since then now alone still she sits
With tears overflowing from her eyes trying to feel me in abyss
Though I am not gone she remembers the vow that I never broke
All around her all that are with her can feel my spirit this I spoke

I'm still here with her in everything she does even to all I do show
I let her know I am sitting beside her as she cries out to my soul
I'm always waiting trying to stop her tears why doesn't she know
As I have vowed I have found her now I am right here it is so!

The night with an entwining kiss when I entered her soul it is known
I have never left this I promised I will never go this she must know
As she sleeps and in her dreams she doesn't feel me as her tears flow
But she doesn't realize as it is her in my arms in her sleep I do hold

It hurts for me to know while I'm here she can't see for I sit beside her
If only she would feel me for I vowed I'd be here and its her I do hold
I told her I'd be near to see me again her shoulders she can look over
For her fears have always been and still are the Destiny of Our Fates

Rose Portillo

When Your Leaves Are Fresh And Green

When Your Leaves Are Fresh And Green,
When Your Trees Are Budding From The Earths;
That Is When You Shall Be Mine Forever

For Your Forever Will Last Just A Little While,
Until Your Stems Are Turning Brown,
And Your Ground Can Share No New Births

There Will No Longer Be Beauty And Loveliness,
Mine Eyes Shall Not Want To Search For Your Loyalty
Nor Will I Find Any Riches Underneath Your Soil

For My Love In Your Eyes Is Only For What Shows
Not The Beauty That Is Lying Underneath My Sighs
I Love You No Longer For No Beauty You've Ever Shown

Picking Your Flowers For They Wilt Now In The Ending Hour
The Witchery Of It All Yet You Think No One Knows
It Will All Be Allright If The Love Stays Within Your Buds

Rose

Depression

This feeling so hurtful so deeply hiding within
Full of melancholic unresolved secret desperation

Seeping way down inside my veins and bones
From even when I can remember thinking unsown

Ever since the memory of this lifetime childhood
All I've known is this lonely mood growing old

It is something no one should ever go through
Nobody should ever have to feel this blue

For when it gets way down inside your blood
There is no escaping from its deadly perilous flood

The silent suffering endured and endless torment
Of drowning tears feeling as if they're waterfall sent

No one will ever really understand or wants to know
The fatal thoughts that each day literally sinking my soul

What an effort it is to continually trying to be all right
To give in to this feeling would be all the devil's delight

But why should I care if I should eventually succumb
The solitary death it inevitably brings so let it be done

There is no one that you can tell me that really cares
This depression is the death of my spirit where will it go?

Rose Portillo

As I Sat

As I Sat In The World You Sent Me To
For What Was The Most Empty Abyss

Oh The Deepest Time When I Went There
Where Were You I Was Crying Out For You!

I Thought You Heard Me When I Left
To Find You In The Never Ever Land Of Death

Yes I Went There And I Really Thought
I Heard You As I Still Listen And I Still Look

Funny I Searched All Over In The Great Fall
Losing In My Mind Though In The Center Of It All

But As I Sat There In Eternity Waiting For You
I Cannot Return Even If Your Promise I Held

I Still Sit I Still Wait For You Unforgotten Within
With The Need To Return To My Heart And My Soul

Minu

To Find

To Find Knowledge And Wisdom
Is To Find Solitude And Pain

To Find Patience And Grace
Is To Find Sufferings Long

To Find Peace And Mercifulness
Is To Find Undoubtedly Mistakes And Errs

To Find Love, Happiness And Pure Joy In One's Heart
Is To Find Forgiveness In Others As Well Within Yourself

And To Find The Greatness Of Pure Love
And Final Safe Haven In Life

Is To Finally Find The Divine Greatness
Of The Heart And Soul

Rose Portillo

Ignorance

Ignorance exists in this world everywhere yes you will find
So many people with their so called "Intelligence" oh so sublime
Oh they will have the knowledge from all the books they read
Still there is no kind of wisdom they're not free in their mind

Ignorance is inside of some of those we don't even know
Eventually though for it doesn't take very long to show
It is sad that it is there for when it comes it has to be gone
How I wish that all people were more like King Solomon

It lies deep down inside people sometimes we won't even see
Lurking everywhere in every household in every corner of every street
Life itself will show if you live long enough to see it come around
Hopefully you will never though oh you will be one of the lucky ones

Ignorance destroys relationships it ruins cities it hurts all in vain
It comes between families hurting brothers and sisters trying to relate
Ignorance is like a disease for there is no cure for it no matter what
It is so hard to know where it lies and it can be hidden causing pain

Be careful you never know where you find this it can be eveywhere
Once you find it you need to know where to get it out it is only right
Ignorance can kill it always causes a wrong deed with the uncaring
It is something that should never be allowed to exist causing fright

I wish I could find it all collect it and get rid of it wherever it lies
Take it and throw it away for it is a sin and it can ruin your life
For ignorance will always cause certain bad things to happen in it
Only the Lord God Himself knows that this should be Good Ridden

Rose

This Darkness

As I Sat Alone In This Horrible Deep Sad Darkness
Wondering How Long The Forever You Said Really Is

As I Sat There Searching For You Suddenly I Began To Cry
I Saw You Standing There Looking For Me I Saw Your Eyes

In This Darkness Of Mine You Were Calling Out My Name!
Inviting Me To Stay In This Darkness That Is Your Comfort Zone

I Called Out To You As You Called Out For Me Maybe Hoping
I Yelled Out Yes But You Turned Away As If You Didn't Hear It

But In This Sad Darkness Of My Heart Where I Still Simply Just Sit
You Don't Hear Me "My Love" As I Try To Call Out Looking For You!

You Left Somewhere I Wait For You To Find Me In This Darkness
I Dwell Inside Of My Own World Here In Hopes Of Me You Will Find

You Don't Come To Me For You Are Stuck In Some Comfort I Realize
So I Sit I Watch You Walk On By In This Other World You Are Still In

Walking Towards The Light You Keep Calling My Name Over And Over
Tried To Touch You Running Calling Your Name But You Turned Away

I Can't Believe You Really Can't Hear My Voice As You Walk On By!
I Call Out While You Walk Right By Me As You Are Still Looking For Me!

You Can't See Me! Don't Let Me Sit In This Darkness I've Come To Be In
I'm Trapped In A Realm As You Live In Another For You Can't Even See Me!

Rose Minu

Loving Someone

Loving Someone So Deeply In Your Heart
Where It Eventually Tears Your Soul Apart
Leaving You Wonder What Kind Of Love Is This
And Where Does This Kind Of Love Originate

Pure Love Is From The Lord For He Has No Hate
Loving Someone Forever Loving Them So Much
To The Extreme When It Literally Physically Hurts
When It Turns Your Insides Inside Out All Distraught

This Kind Of Love Has And Can Create Strange Emotions
To The Extreme Of Hating That Someone Filled With Pain
Causing One To Wonder If Love Is Really From Heaven At All
For Feelings So Awful Cannot Be Sent From Up Above

For Pure Love Would Never Want To Hurt So Badly
If Love Can Render The Tearing Of Souls This Tough
Seems To Me That Love Like This Is Not Really Love
For It Begins From Oneself Selfish It Is Conceitedly Sad

All That Is Touched By This Grand Kind Of Love Transparent
Seeming To Become Broken And Torn To Pieces Hurting All
All Seeming Good Finally Becoming Deceitfully Obsessed About
What Sort Of Love Hurts If It Does Not Fulfill Anyone's Needs

Rose

I Know It's Over

It's hard to be there when you still want to go
Does it hurt you to be there? But when will I go?

I know it took me a while to understand and really see
You were always there I'm so sorry I didn't know

I just didn't believe that you wanted to leave
Why didn't you just say you really truly wanted to go?

Okay allright I guess I know it's over for us then
But it's was so hard getting it started our life to begin

Well I hope that without me you have a nice life to live
I'm sorry that it was so hard for you to show love to me

That all we had to be for each other was just friends
We would have made it that way forever I believe

How sad that there's bitterness and hatred in between
Instead of kindness and love which says so I know it's over

Rose Portillo

It Happened So Long Ago

His Last Stand Happened So Very Very Long Ago
They Shot Him Down But They Took My soul

All He Wanted To Do Was To Make Me His Wife
I Played With Him When I Was Only Six Years Old

We Were Children Together Is All That I Can Remember
His Face So Beautiful His Voice He Always Sang To Me

The Way That He Loved Me So Much Was So Unbelievable!
Everyone Would Always Say That We Were Destined To Be

It Was Written In The Books For Him And I To Be As One
But When I Was Thirteen He Finalized Me Being His Girl

I Knew Within My Heart That Nothing Would Ever Change
I Said Inside My Self That I Knew I Would Always Be His

A Dreadful Day Was When Those Guys Just Took His Life Away
Why Him God? Why The One Who Loves And Adores Only Me

I'm Sorry But Why Didn't They Take Someone Else That Day
I Feel Selfish But You Know I Am Going To Be Left All Alone!

Now I Am Here This Day With Him Gone It Happened So Long Ago
No One To Sing To Me The Way He Did No One To Love Me!

It Happened So Very Long Ago Though It Seems Just Like Yesterday
When They Stole His Life From This World And They Just Took Him Away!

Rose Portillo

This is for Rudy Saenz (My Beautiful Love, which began at childhood; at the age
of 6, whose life was stolen with a gun from a life style that was not his from a gang
life that he didn't belong to!)

How You Make Me Feel

I Never Thought You'd Make Me Feel
The Way I Feel About You Tonight
I Loved You So Much At One Time
You Had No Clue How I Was So For Reals

You Had Me In The Palm Of Your Hands
So Ignorant I Was Of Your Hatred Ways Unseen
The More I Showed You Love The Meaner You Became
You Would Become My Worst Enemy Even In My Bed

The Stories Had Been Told To Me About You
They Told Me How Little You Cared Of Anyone At All
So Don't Blame Me When I Wonder What's True
When You Would Make Any Argument To Leave Me

You Made It Plain It Was Me You Didn't Like Anymore
But I Can't Believe You Now Make Me Feel It's Unreal
How My Love Could Be There So Strong Now It's Gone
It Hurts To Know You've Been The One So Hateful All Along!

Rose Portillo

So Evil So Mean So Cruel

How could they want him to stay mad to be so mean so evil and cruel,
If they love him wouldn't they want him to be the best person he could?

Don't they see the love he has in his heart how he has his own mind?
Do they want him to pretend his love does not exist just so they could insist?

Take a good look at him his heart and think of his happiness for once,
How could they just want him to hate someone he just wants to Love?

If they love him they will realize without her he'll be more lost than before?
Will they just keep blaming someone else for the problems he helped cause

Do they want him to act like a little boy instead of facing life continuing to try?
Hello? He is a grown man not a child not a girl and certainly not a little boy!

He is a married man who made mistakes also for it always takes two,
Of course he won't tell them exactly what he did to help make it go wrong!

That doesn't mean that their marriage failed all because of the actions of one,
He is responsible for marrying her in front of God and at fault for the break up of
it too!

Everyone deserves to be happy if they wish and decide to try to work at being one,
They deserve to try at their marriage especially if it is for God's Vows that were
done.

You can't teach him to Honor a Promise made to God then get angry if he does,
Then convince him that mistakes are not to be forgiven if he is to be forgiven
himself?

What advise would be given to them if it were their marriage that was involved?
Who would hold it against them to forgive their loved one of any wrong?

Someone needs to stop him from blaming others for what he was also a part of,
If you love him then help him show him that his Marriage comes first that is Love

Instead of dogging it down making him feel that trying for it should not be done,
Take a good look at yourselves your hearts with love instead of selfishness even
still!

Do not pressure <u>your</u> anger and push on him only what <u>you</u> want him to do,
For your parents would encourage to Forgive to Love not be evil mean or cruel!

Rose Portillo

Love Deeper

ALL THAT WAS ON THE OUTSIDE WORLD WAS NEVER UNTOLD
THAT WON'T TOUCH WHAT WAS BETWEEN OUR TWO SOULS

DEEPEST REVELATIONS FOUND WISDOM ONCE WE HAD SPOKE
TRUE LOVE PLEASURES ALWAYS ASSUMED WE BOTH HAD FOUND

NOTHING COULD NEVER COMPARE TO ALL THAT WAS ON FACE
FOR WHAT WE ALL SEE IS ONLY ON THE OUTSIDE COVER PAGE

BUT WHAT WE SHARED DISCOVERIES OF GLORY AND GRACE
TOGETHER SOUGHT WE FELT ONLY WHAT TWO COULD HAVE
KNOWN

I THOUGHT WE WERE MORE THAN ALL THAT CAN BE TRACED
IT WAS DEEPER THAN JUST TWO LIVES THAT COULDN'T BE FELT

WHAT IS SO BEAUTIFUL IS WHAT ALONG THE WAY WE HAD
FOUND
US IN THE DEPTH OF LIFE'S LOVE DEEPER THAN WE HAD
ALLOWED

THE PRETENSE OF THEIRS TRULY INDEED WAS WHAT OURS WAS
NOT
THERE IS A LOVE DEEPER AND MORE THAN WHAT IS NOT SHOWN

ROSE PORTILLO

Come Back Home

Remember When You Loved Me,
When Everything Was Sweet And Good?

Remember When I Was A Joy To See,
When You Adored Every Step I Took?

Remember When I Would Cry To You,
When You Would No One Let Hurt Me?

What Happened To Those Days Untold,
Where Did All Those Wonderful Times Go?

Where Did My Best Friend Leave To,
Ask Them Why Couldn't I Too Go?

Why Did They Have To Take Only You,
Why Couldn't They Take Me Too?

Everyone Knows How Much I Need Your Soul,
That My Heart Would Die Alone In The Cold?

Now Here I Am Looking For You All Alone
You Who Loved Me You Were Like Gold

Tell Them Please To Let You Come Back,
So That You Can Finally Come Back Home.

Rose Portillo

Could It Possibly Be

Could it possibly be,
That it is You standing near me
By my side but still I could not see
All along all of this time I knew

Could it possibly be,
That you were always the one
That it was you who never forgot
And it is through he you are not gone

Could it possibly be,
That is the only reason why
You stood so deep in my heart
Because he in the ground he does lie

Could it possibly be,
That he is "Our Angel"
That from him you were guided
For the messenger of us to see

Could it possibly be, that
Although he loved me too
It is all supposed to be true
For the love to forego for me and you

Could it possibly be, then
For without his beautiful soul
It would never had been known
The love between us now to be told

With Love,
From Minu

As I Sit Here

As I Sit Here In My Heart I Feel I'm Beside You
That Look In Your Eyes Yet You Are So Far Away
The Sadness Shows Still Through Your Disguise

I Can See The Pain That Was Hiding Deep Inside
Burning Hurting All The While Yet I Ask Why
For Wherever He Is With You My Heart Still Lies

I Still Feel Your Fear Longing With The Aches
That You Felt So Deep Within You Back Then
Your Soul Of Love Filled Now With All My Tears

I Give You My Love Never Seeming Real To Me
My Heart Is All I Hold While I Sit I Wait For You
The Way He Is A Part Of Me Giving His Love To Be

Though My Aching Shame Cannot Cure My Broken Heart
To Even Try To Erase The Pain I Caused You To Feel Inside
With My Blanket Of Love Covering Over Again I Just Sigh

As I Sit Here With The Craving Pangs Of Loss I Feel
The Urge To Heal All The Pain Your Tears No Longer Cry
Knowing It Will Be Only With Our Love That I Try To Find

Trying To Comfort Your Hurt Remaining No Longer A Role
With Your Haunting Memories Creased Inside Trying To Unfold
Surely Only To Uncover More Truth Right From Under Your Soul

Rose Minu Portillo

Don't You Know

Don't You Know That She Still Sits All Alone
In The Middle Of Nowhere Waiting For You To Come Home

Don't You Know That It Was You All Along Living For Her
Only You Held The Key To Her Heart's Will To Live

Now That They Have Taken You Away From Along Her Side
To The Unknown World You Are In She Is Still Living Alone

There She Just Sits Although You Can Go See For Yourself
You'll See That There Is A Wildflower Struggling Trying To Grow

You Are The Water That She So Desperately Is Without
You Are What Is Needed For Her Beautiful Petals To Bloom

Don't You Know She Sits Where No One Can Believe
Is Where She Still Waits For The Light Of Her Love To See

You Are The Light Of Her Love The Air That She Breathes
For She Struggles Each Day To Stay Where She Can Seed

The Wildflower Of Yours You Loved So Much Needs Your Arms
Don't You Know That She Is Still There Waiting For You

It's Been Years Suffering For She Is Trying Hard To Stay Alive
Trying And Pretending Where She Lives She Doesn't Belong

Don't You Know Without You Though She Will Die Soon Enough
Without The Only Key To Her Soul But It's You That Has The Clue

She Waits For You To Go See Her To Hold Her Once More Again
Go To Her Water Her Please Save Her Loneliness Give Her Your Song

Don't You Know That It Is For Only You That She Will Forever Long
The Presence Of Your Love Is Pure Gold Precious For Her Growth

Rose Minu

184

Eirene

EIRENE, IN THAT ONE LIFE I HAD TO LIVE
IT WAS ONLY YOU MY NEWBORN THERE FOR ME,

FOR ME TO CONTINUE TO STAY STRONG AND BEAUTIFUL
THE LIGHT YOU BROUGHT WHEN YOU CRIED FOR MY LOVE,

I, BLINDLY STRUGGLING WITH NO URGE TO GO ON,
YOU CHANGED MY HEART AS I HELD YOU IN MY ARMS,

BEGGING FOR THE STRENGTH MY BABE FOR IT WAS ME IN NEED
FROM WITHIN I COULDN'T SEE IT WAS YOU HE SENT TO ME

SO HEARTBROKEN AS I SAT THERE AND CRIED WITH YOU
YEARNING HURT SO BAD NEEDING DESPERATELY TO LEAVE,

THEN AS I AWOKE FROM A BAD DREAM AS YOU I FEED
ALONE WITHOUT ME COULD I REALLY LET YOU BE?

YOUR TEARS SO FILLED INSIDE YOUR TINY BEAUTIFUL EYES
CRIED OUT TO ME AS IF FOR MY SOUL TO PLEASE RETURN,

YOU GAVE ME BACK THE JOY THAT I BORE YOU IN
GIVING BACK THE STRENGTH THAT I HAD SO DRAINED,

AND YOU MY BEAUTIFUL TINY SOUL GIFT OF GOD FOR ME
I WILL SAVE MY STRENGTH YOU GAVE TO GIVE TO YOU,

WHEN YOU TOO SOON ENOUGH IN THE LIFE YOU'LL LEAD
WILL NEED IN HARDSHIPS THAT YOU CRY SILENTLY FOR.

YOUR MOTHER

How Do I

How Do I Stop These Tears
From Falling From My Eyes

How Do I Erase This Pain
I'm Feeling Deep Down Inside

How Do I Tell My Heart
Not To Feel The Pain Being Torn Apart

How Do I Still Pretend
You Never Existed There Is No End

How Do I Go On
Now That You Are Gone

How Do I Confess That I Lost
A Dream That Went All Wrong

How Do I Lie To Myself
That You Never Held Me Close

How Do I Forget
The Memory Of You Lingering Still

How Do I Tell Them How Much I Love You
So Much That You Stole My Soul

So Tell Me Now,
How Do I Remain In This World
How Do I Exist I Will Try I Suppose

Rose Portillo

How I Wish

How I Wish You Would Have Smiled That Day
That One Day When I First Saw You Standing There

How I Wish I Would Have Followed My Instincts
When I Wanted To Make You A Part Of My Life

How I Wish You Would Have Only Said Hello To Me
Each Time I Caught You Gazing Deep In My Eyes

How I Wish You Could Have Seen Me Looking Back At You
All The While Contemplating On What I Should Do

How I Wish All These Years Would Have Been With You
For I Always Remembered And Thought About You

How I Wish I Would Have Not Turned My Shoulder
It Seems That I Was Always Just Around The Other Corner

How I Wish I Could Have Helped You With All Your Fears
Then You Would Have Known It Is I To Dry Your Tears

How I Wish The Lord Would Have Shown Me Sooner
Wait A Minute . . . . He Did I Did Not Know How Foolish I Was

How I Wish I Would Have Noticed More Than Your Stares
That You Were There Always Here Always Everywhere

How I Wish That You Would Have Not Been So Shy
You Would Have Seen That Waiting For You All Along Was I

Rose Portillo

187

This Pain Time Cannot Heal

This pain I carry inside is not the kind you can see
If you look real close you'll miss it but please believe

It's been hidden deep for so many many years
Every mention of what it holds cannot erase the tears

It hurts when I laugh no matter what you try
I cannot hold it in any longer I don't know why

It hurts so bad no one can heal the very cause
It's taken so many years just to know how I lost

Time I thought might hold the magic key for me
To even out the score of the pain that lies so deep

Now it's been over a decade of broken sad smiles
It's in my blood it's determined not to go any miles

My only hope and dream is what this might hold for me
Is the breath to my soul of only your loving healing

But it is as I have always feared is what I've been told
There is no cure for this pain that my painful body still holds

For this pain time itself cannot possibly ever even heal
All the hurt and suffering I feel believe me is for real

Rose Portillo

Please Tell God

DO YOU THINK, FOR ME YOU CAN PLEASE TELL GOD
I DIDN'T MEAN TO HURT YOU SO BADLY THE WAY I DID

IT WASN'T ON MY MIND TO HURT ANYONE ESPECIALLY YOU
I WANTED JUST TO HAVE YOUR LOVE AND BE LOVED TOO

I REALLY THOUGHT IF I LEFT YOU WITH ENOUGH TIME
YOU'D BE OKAY AND EVERYTHING FOR US WOULD BE FINE

I KNOW I AM A BIG GIRL I CAN'T BLAME ANYONE BUT MYSELF
BLAMING THE LACK OF TRUTH FOR ALL THAT HAPPENED TO
YOU

BEING IGNORANT THINKING I KNEW THAT I COULD FIX IT ALL
HOPING I WAS RIGHT ABOUT THE FUTURE WAS WHAT I SAW

BELIEVING IF YOU MET SOMEONE SHE'D MAKE YOU FORGET
SOMEONE COULD LOVE ME LIKE YOU I'M PLAYING RUSSIAN
ROULLET

YEAH RIGHT NO ONE LOVED ME NOT THE WAY THAT YOU EVER
DID
YES AND I KNOW SHE WOULDN'T EVER MAKE YOU FORGET ME

SO CAN YOU FOR ME PLEASE TELL GOD I'M REALLY TRULY SORRY
FOR ALL YOUR PAIN I CAUSED FOR NOT COMING BACK THAT DAY

HE GAVE YOU TO ME FROM THE BEGINNING AND ALWAYS DID
AGAIN
HE KNOWS HOW MUCH YOU LOVE ME IT'S SO MUCH THE WAY HE
DOES

SO AGAIN I BEG YOU PLEASE PLEASE TELL GOD TO FORGIVE ME
FOR NOT BEING WITH YOU THAT DAY YOU LEFT I WANTED TO GO
TOO

PLEASE TELL GOD I LOVE YOU TO PLEASE LET YOU KEEP LOVING
ME
TELL GOD I MISS YOU THAT FOREVER AND ETERNITY I'LL BE
SORRY!

ROSE PORTILLO

She Said She Killed You

She was there that day you were buried in the ground
She was dressed in all black as was common for all
She wouldn't speak or look at anyone straight in their eyes
Quietly she hugged everyone with apologies but she didn't cry

Shocked left in a daze you could see she didn't know what to do
Everyone seen you together when you both were so very young
Only then she seemed happy playing all the time with you
But that day there was a lost far away look in her eyes so long

We talked all night about how much you wanted her for your wife
Loneliness seemed to be the friend she found alone with me that night
I sat with her I wanted to be a part of you through her it felt right
She wouldn't laugh she wouldn't smile with you she wanted to go

There was such a quiet sadness inside yes she missed your love
Her eyes told the story how she would die without you just to be with you
So either way there was no choice in her sad heart except not to go on
She said she killed you it was her fault but to her you were not gone

She would change her mind quite often she seemed so unable to cry
For her denial was in what she knew but what she just wouldn't say
She did say you had been waiting for her and that she was coming home!
She said you were looking for her that you thought she was forever gone!

Then she said she tried to get rid of him for you and he beat her so bad!
She cried out she was coming home then you thought she left you alone
She was angry with someone who told you to forget her what a friend
She says she killed you because she came home too late she took too long

I loved her that night instantly I knew I saw what you loved about her
She loved you so so much she wanted to die with you oh she wanted to go
I got her to smile I saw what you saw in her I don't know how I knew
Talking about you all night I wished to go find you to bring you back home

I wanted to see you to tell you just how lucky you had been to have her love
She asked why you left her she never wanted to stay here in this ugly world alone
She wanted only to go with you to be by your side wherever you were though
I wanted to go with you too why did you leave us both here in this world so cold!

I felt the hurt in her heart wondering why and for you brother I'd carry her along
She needed you so much it showed right through I could see all of her awful pain
I missed you so much that night then she said she killed you I told her it wasn't
true
We talked all night she drank with me we cried she said to her you'd never be
gone!

My Frozen Heart

MY HEART FROZE MY MIND LOST ALL LOGICAL REASONING
I COULDN'T FIND YOU I LOOKED FOR YOU I WAITED TOO
I LOOKED EVERYWHERE I ASKED EVERYONE IF THEY KNEW
THEY TOLD ME I NEEDED TO GO ON TO FORGET ABOUT YOU

MY MIND WAS FAR AWAY ALL THE TIME WITH NOTHING LEFT
THE ONLY HEART I HAD LEFT HAD BEEN TAKEN WITH YOU
HE WENT TO THE THE DEPTHS OF NEVER TO FIND HIS LOVE
BUT IT WAS OVER FOR ME ONLY MY BODY WAS LEFT TO EXIST

YOU SAID YOU'D TAKE CARE OF IT ALL WELL WHAT YOU LIED?
YOU BECAME ANGRY IMPATIENT FOR WHAT SOMEONE ELSE SAID?
YOU REMEMBERED THE HEARTBREAK BELIEVING ANOTHER
FOOL
I'M STILL HERE I'M WAITING FOR YOU TO COME FOREVER MORE!

YOUR LADY MINU

A Beautiful Angel Boy

BORN OF THE SPIRITS FROM THE KINDEST OF SOULS
TRULY PRAYED FOR FROM THE HEARTS OF GOLD

HIS FATHER IS THE ONLY FATHER WE HAVE FROM ABOVE
PRAYED PROPHETED FOR SURE FROM THE ANGEL'S HE'D COME

SWEETEST LITTLE ANGEL MAN HE CAME IS WHAT GOD GAVE TO
ME
FOR FEAR OF MY LOSS OF MY LOVE WHO FORGOT TO TAKE ME
TOO

SO INSTEAD HE LEFT ME THE MOST BEAUTIFUL ANGEL MALE SON
AS ALL THE LOVE HE HELD HE GAVE HIS HEART THROUGH MY
SON ALONE

For my son, Benny Boy . . . .

ROSE PORTILLO

Too Little Too Late

EXPECTED TOO MUCH FROM HIM MAYBE EVEN TOO SOON
THE MAN COULDN'T AND DOESN'T KNOW HOW TO LOVE
ANYONE

NO LOVE WAS TO BE TOO MUCH BUT SO MUCH INSIDE WAS PRIDE
THAT WAS ALL HE HAD AND LEARNED SO HE NEVER TRIED

NO LOVE BEFORE ALIVE JUST INSECURITY YES WAS JUST BORN
LONELINESS I LIVED WITH HIM THEN NOW BECAUSE I STILL LIVE

CAN'T LEAVE ME BUT DON'T LOVE ME SO NO ONE REALLY CARES
LET IT GO THEY SAY FOR ALL HE WANTS FROM YOU IS REVENGE

TOO SAD MISERABLE I MUST SAY THIS MUCH FOR I'VE HAD
ENOUGH
NOT EVEN TOO LATE FOR THERE HAS TO BE LOVE TO BE TOO
LATE

NOT ENOUGH LOVE TO BE TOO LITTLE THEN TOO LATE ALWAYS
I'M TIRED FOR TOO MUCH TODAY STILL TOO SAD TOO MUCH
HATE

ROSE PORTILLO

My Wildflower-My Lady

SHE WAS EVERYTHING EVEN MORE THAN EVERYTHING TO ME
THEY ALL JUST HAD NO CLUE NO THEY JUST COULD NOT SEE
THEY DID NOT KNOW HER HEART HER BEAUTIFUL WAYS TOO
ALL THEY SAW OF HER WAS SADNESS AND HER HATRED FOR FOOLS

I LOVED HER AT FIRST SIGHT SHE WAS MY SIGHT FOR SORE EYES
I KNOW SHE LOVED ME IT SHOWED RIGHT THROUGH HER HEART
IT WAS IN HER SWEET SEXY SMILE SHE GAVE TO ME ALL THE TIME
IN HER NOD TO ME AS SHE WAS TRYING TO BE HARD YET SO CUTE

PRETTY AS A ROSE HER GOOD HEART WAS ALL SHE HAD TO LIVE
SO MUCH OF HER BEAUTY SCARED ALMOST ALL OF THE OTHER
GUYS
SHE WAS MY WILDFLOWER MY LADY WITH SO MUCH LOVE TO GIVE
SHE WAS ALWAYS MY SPECIAL LADY SHE WILL ALWAYS BE IN MY
EYES

I TOLD HER I ADORED HER AND HER SMILE BRIGHTENED MY DAYS
EACH TIME SHE LEFT I WOULD TAKE HER BACK AGAIN YES EVERY
TIME
EVEN THOUGH SHE WOULD ALWAYS RUNAWAY SHE KNEW SHE WAS
MINE
IT'S OKAY I KNEW WHY SHE HID HER LOVE FOR ME I JUST KNEW
HER WAYS

SO TOUGH ON THE OUTSIDE YET SO TENDER SO BEAUTIFUL INSIDE
LIKE THAT
NOT VERY MANY PEOPLE WERE EVEN BLESSED TO BE WITH HER
LONG ENOUGH
TO KNOW HER THE WAY I DID TO BE IN HER LIFE EVEN WITH HER
SMILE SO BLUE
I THANKED GOD EACH DAY FOR GIVING HER TO ME TO LOVE NO
MATTER WHAT

SHE WAS MY LADY MY HEART MY BABY MY PRETTY EYES AND MY
QUEEN
I WAS THE LOVE OF HER LIFE HER SWEETHEART AND YES I WAS
HER KING
I KNOW SHE LOVED ME IT WAS IN HER EYES IT ALWAYS SHOWED I
AM SO SURE
SHE LEFT FOR FEAR OF ALL WHO HURT AND HATED HER TRYING TO
STOP OUR LOVE

HER WILD SPIRIT I KNEW THROUGH HER LOVING CHILDLIKE
SECRETLY FUN HEART
SO KIND BEING SO SWEET ALWAYS READY TO COME AND STAND
BESIDE ME
WHATEVER I WANTED AND STANDING BY MY SIDE NEVER WANTING
TO BE APART
I LOVED THAT ABOUT HER YES I LOVED MY LADY MY BEAUTIFUL
WILDFLOWER

IN THE STILL OF NIGHT SHE ASKED ME IF I THOUGHT SHE WAS A
LADY TO ME
I SMILED FOR SHE HAD ALWAYS BEEN A LADY IN EVERY SENSE AND
YES SO PRETTY
EVEN WHEN SHE WAS ANGRY AT ME FOR PLAYING AROUND AND
BEING WRONG
I SMILED SHE CRIED SCARED BUT SHE WAS MY HEART MY LADY MY
WILDFLOWER

TONY COTA

One Man

One Man's Joy Is Another Man's Sorrow
One Man Laughs While Another Man Cries
Carrying A Love Both Willing To Die For

Whether Or Not Who's Right For Either Might Be Wrong
No One Cares Enough For A Second Chance At Tomorrow
If They Tried To End It Instead Living It Through A Song

Can It Be That One Man's Love Is Another Man's Folly
What One Man Cannot Do Without The Love Of His Life
Will He Give It All Away Remaining In His Melancholy

As One Man's Strength Can Be The Other Man's Weakness
Will One Man Let It All Go Just To Let Another Man Be Great
As One Man's Sadness Can Become The Other Man's Glee

All To Hold Her Beauty In The Palm Of The One's Hand
To Have His Love's Sweetness Even If To Be Betrayed
Befriending All For The Soft Loving Touch Forever Sweet

Yes Indeed What Can Be One Man's Love Is One Man's Toil
The Difference In What One Man Wants While One Man Strays
We All Die A Little With Only One Man's Wounds Cutting Away

But Try To Tell This To A Man Who's Heart Is Stolen Forever
It Is Like Speaking To A Cold Wall Not Knowing It Is His Foil
Better To Die With Love In His Heart Than To Remain Alive Soiled

Rose Portillo

Just An Illusion

Was it just a night's fantasy or simply a dream?
A "Magical Moment" kept in the "Forever Scheme,"
After that summer maybe it was just a daydream
That could never have been reality or really been?

Forever this lingers it stays since in the beginning
So very long ago though through the ages I say,
As if it is on hold through time still just lingering
Among the midsts of "Lost Loves" dwelling therein.

When everything around me was always what I felt
So pure of his essence around me just like "Heaven,"
Only to be seen and be with me in this physical realm
Knowing that our future is what perished instead.

So who was I to dare to believe you were there
That I even existed with your love before then?
Frozen is not our hearts but who were you back then
To dread me leaving yet ironically it is I still here!

All of it I could have sworn was right in front of us
For all of the universe and all people to see too,
Yet not one entity would admit to our love our presence
Let them carry my spirit my soul and love back to you?

Only you can hold onto my heart "Forever and a Day"
Taking my life with it for time has stood still for me,
It seems we will never cross the barrier of dimensions
Hence will our love and spirits ever again be together free?

Please you angels I do plea do it for me for I cannot reach
That one "Magical Moment" that remains always for keeps,
Keeping me wherever you want is where I still wait to be
Though I cannot find you no matter how hard I try to see

Stuck in between worlds that hold us spiritually together
Yet no one knows what happens with Love that is "Forever,"
Extremely anxiously stuck with this "Forever Love of Mine"
Waiting for you but it has been so long yet only a second to find!

Will I ever see your sweet smile and beautiful face again?
Will you ever be by my side to hold me once again?
Do I belong? I can't find even myself "My Angel of Mine?"
Ironically you were trying to find me for I was stuck in time

I'm waiting for the chance to step into your realm again
Back into your eyes which told me of your "True Love,"
While your spirit holds onto the key to that "Magic Moment"
Feeling again our love that cannot be really ever known again

My dream is for you to come back to me in this my reality
To love me again as no one ever has and ever will but you,
Although this love has been kept secret and now forever lost
"The Forever Realm" which must have been "Just An Illusion!"

Rose Portillo

Red Is A Rose

The pain in his heart shows no blood being shed
But the bright candy apples shining are oh so red

Oh yes, tomorrow could bring some red roses instead
And for all we know is that we carry love's dread

This life isn't nice until you see a beautiful sunset
With orange purplish color with deep red inside of it

So happy she was the day he brought her his love
Only now the color red represents roses from above

Cherries in the snow is the saying how it goes
More red than tomatoes his love the more it grows

Only for him and her was that beautiful red sky
Thee red rose for their love lingering in the night

It felt so good to know for their love Red Rose so true
For the light of the night before the red dawns for Rose soon

Rose is her name hoping the future holds no more being apart
Now it goes without saying their love's red in the heart

Rose Portillo

A Door

A Door leading you to a place never known,
Unless you open it this place can be the beach,
Where the water sinks into the sand or,
The Rain Forest where the birds sing in the trees,
A Door can lead you anywhere and you'll never know.

If you were led into a rain forest and,
A bird talks to you as you walk by,
You listen closely, he says to you "Don't cry."
And then you say, "Why shouldn't I?"
The bird says, "Everything will be alLright."
You walk away from the talking bird,
And you think about what you just heard,
Then you look into the sky,
You see the sun and it looks back at you,
And it says, "I love you and you are with me,
There is no need to cry for you opening The Door
Which leads to me right under my wing."

Desiree Grace

The me I used to be

I used to hate vegetables
But now I love my greens
I used to be short
But now I'm tall
I used to think my parent's knew everything
But now I realize they don't
I used to want to be a teacher
But now I want to be a psychologist
I used to want to play the drums
But now I play the guitar
I used to like toys
But now I like to go to the movies
I used to want to be 10
But now I can't wait to be 14

Desiree Grace

I am

Love, giving, faithful

Honesty is important to me

Loyalty is important to me

Unselfishness is important to me

Having faith is important

Analytical is bad but can help

You can be prudent

The world is getting weaker

I'm getting stronger

People are too ignorant

This is me . . . Desiree Grace

I Am

I AM SWEET AND FUNNY
I WONDER WHAT HEAVEN'S LIKE
I HEAR LAUGHING LEPRACHAUNS
I SEE PEGASUS'
I WANT TO BE A SINGER
I AM SWEET AND FUNNY

I PRETEND I'M A SINGER
I FEEL LOST IN A CLOUD
I TOUCH THE STARS
I WORRY ABOUT MY FAMILY
I CRY FOR MY MOM
I AM SWEET AND FUNNY

I UNDERSTAND MY MOM IS SICK
I SAY GOD IS LOVE
I DREAM OF BEING A SINGER
I TRY TO LIVE IN GOD'S WORD
I HOPE THERE'S A CURE FOR MY MOM
I AM SWEET AND FUNNY

PRINCESS ANNA

O, Chocolate Ice Cream

HOW I MISS YOUR CHOCOLATE TASTE

ON THE EDGE OF MY CRAVING TONGUE

AS I THINK BACK ON ALL THOSE YEARS

ENJOYING YOU SO MUCH WHEN I WAS YOUNG

REMEMBERING O, CHOCOLATE ICE CREAM IN TEARS

THE FUDGE STILL LEFT ON MY FINGERS FROM THE STICK

KNOWING THE LOVE OF YOU HAS BEEN NO DREAM

REGARDLESS OF THE DRIPPING CHOCOLATE OH SO THICK

REMINISCING AND WISHING FOR YOUR TASTE ONCE AGAIN

PRINCESS ANNA

How I Love You Mom

How I love you mom so true

As I see you clearly in my mind still

And the yester years of your beauty

Still mesmerizing forever it seems

My love for you always so unconditional

To this day no wrong has ever been

Wishing your love for me is the same

Returning good with memories of your smiles

Taking away only time from my days

To sit in beautiful memories of how I love you

Princess Anna

My Orange Poem

The outside is bumpy like a bumpy road
That leads to nowhere
The outside is round and orange like the
Sun on a hot summer day

The orange is round like an orange
Bouncy ball
The orange is like the sun in the hot
Desert

On the inside the orange smelled
Like a tropical rain forest
The inside was like a burst
Of bright sunshine

One bite of the orange and it's like
Fireworks in the sky

Princess Anna

There once was a boy who was rude

He was always in a very bad mood

Only one thing would make him happy

That was for his Pappy

To give him his only favorite food

There once was a man from Tennessee

This man liked to drink a lot of tea

One day he was so loaded

That he just exploded

And everyone wanted to see that man from Tennessee

Princess Anna

In my lovely yard
Nice beautiful flowers grow
Each lovely spring day

In the nice blue sky
Birds soar to seek adventure
Each hot summer day

In a green cacoon
A caterpillar waits to
Be a butterfly

Princess Anna

Today Is A Good Day For Love

TODAY IS A GOOD DAY FOR LOVE
ALL BECAUSE IT COMES FROM UP ABOVE

THE SMILES OF ANGELS DANCING IN THE SKIES
I SEE THE SPARKLES FROM THE STARS IN HER EYES

AS MY BEAUTIFUL DAUGHTER'S JOY SPINS IN MY HEAD
HER LOVE FOR ME WILL STAY LONG AFTER I'M DEAD

FOR SHE TWIRLS AND TWIRLS WITH LAUGHTER AGAIN
AS MY LOVE FOR HER IS TRULY FROM GOD HEAVEN SENT

MY LOVE FOR HER SO STRONG IT CAN SURELY NEVER END
AS SHE SMILES IT HURTS ME FOR IT IS SO OFTEN UNSAID

FOR ME TELL HER I LOVE HER OH YOU ANGELS ABOVE HER
AS YOU DANCE WITH HER DAILY ALL AROUND HER HEAD

GIVE HER THE SWEET WORDS IN HER MIND THAT I SAY
AND GIVE HER ALL OF MY LOVE EACH AND EVERY DAY

FOR NOT ALWAYS WILL I BE HERE TO HOLD HER HANDS
SO I KISS HER ON HER FOREHEAD AS I WIPE HER TEARS

I TELL HER TO SING AND DANCE EVEN WHEN I'M GONE
FOREVER I WILL BE NEAR HER I WILL NEVER LEAVE HER SIDE

LET ME DANCE WITH THE ANGELS AS SHE WILL FEEL ME SAY
THEN AS I DANCE TO HEAVEN FOR LOVE IT WILL BE A GOOD DAY

I WILL BRUSH HER HAIR SOFTLY THEN SHE WILL KNOW TO
DANCE
FOREVER I WILL STAY WITH HER I WILL BE HER ANGEL FROM
ABOVE

From Rose Portillo to her daughter Princess Anna

Desiree Grace

CURLS BEAUTIFUL ROUND WITH BROWN TWINKLING EYES
FOREVER SINGING TALKING AND MAKING ALL OF US SMILE

SHE WAS A DREAM COME TRUE FOR THE FAMILY ALL THE WHILE
SHE KEPT US ALL HAPPY LAUGHING SHE BROUGHT US TO LIFE

POSSIBLY BORN SO AS WE OUGHT NOT HAVE THE BLUES
TRUE TO HER NAME AS GRACE DANCES AWAY ALL BAD MOODS

SHE WAS THE LIFE OF ALL OF US HER BEAUTY HAD BEEN DREAMT
YES SHE WAS A LIVING DOLL AS EVERYONE HAD ALL SAID

OUR PRAYERS WERE ANSWERED AT LAST SHE HAD BEEN BORN
SHE NEEDED HER SISTER PRINCESS THOUGH EVENLY ADORNED

ALONG THE NEXT LINE WAS MY PRINCESS ANNA A PRETTY FAIR
SHE LOVED HER SO MUCH TOGETHER THEY ARE PERFECT PAIR

THE ANGELS BLESSED HER WITH LA-LA WHEN SHE WAS BORN
THE MOST BEAUTIFUL CURLY HAIR BOUNCING EVERY MORN

FOR SHE WAS TRULY A SWEETIE AND YES ONLY GOD KNEW
HER BEAUTY WOULD BE SO BOUNTIFUL YES SHE WAS SO CUTE

I LOVE MY DESIREE GRACE SO MUCH DEAR LORD GOD ITS TRUE
TELL HER I LOVE HER STAY TRUE AND TELL HER TO BE GOOD

HER HEART IS REAL AND SHE HAS SO MUCH LOVE TO GIVE
DESIREE GRACE YOUR BEAUTY HAS BECOME INNER BEAUTY TOO

STAY BEAUTIFUL INSIDE AND PLEASE DON'T EVER CHANGE
FOR YOU WILL FOREVER MAKE US SMILE AS I DANCE WITH YOU

LOVE YOU NEED YOU, WANT YOU TO STAY THE YOU THAT IS
GOOD
GOD LOVES YOU DESIREE GRACE AND YES YOUR MAMA TOO!

I LOVE YOU DESIREE, MOM

Mercy Girl

SUCH A WARM LOVING PINK BEAUTY WAS BORN
CRYING THE SECOND I WOKE FROM THEM CUTTING MY WOMB

FEELING LIKE IF FOREVER WAS TRYING TO TAKE HER
PLEADING FOR EVERYONE TO GET MY BABY FOR ME TO CARE

SHE WAS BORN WITH ME LONGING TO HOLD CONSTANTLY
ONTO THE ANGELS AS THEY CREATED FROM MY LOVING SOUL

AS IF SHE WAS SO BEAUTIFULLY PINK THAT IT COULDN'T BE
NEVER TRYING TO DESTROY THE BEAUTIFUL HEAVENLY SENT

FOREVER LOVING THE CHILD OF GOD I NAMED HER MERCY
THE PICTURE OF AN ANGEL IN PINK FOR SHE'S GOD'S PRETTY

MERCY GIRL I LOVE YOU MORE THAN YOU'LL EVER KNOW
THE BABY OF TWELVE BUT NEVER THE LAST OF MY LOVES

THE LAST IS THE FIRST IN ALL THAT KARMA COMES AROUND
HOWEVER WE LOVE IN THIS WORLD THEY ARE FOREVER LOVED
ALL

MERCY IS WHAT BEAUTY DID GIVEN HER EVEN IN CHARACTER
THE MEANING OF HER NAME IS WHAT I KNOW SHE WILL STAY

FOREVER REMEMBERING THAT I ALMOST LOST MY GIRL MERCY
MAKES HER LIFE SO SPECIAL BRINGING ALL OF US LOVE'S WAY

THE MOST PRECIOUS SPECIAL BABY OF MINE THE LORD GAVE TO
ME
A SPECIAL TASK OF LOVE SHOWING JUST HOW MUCH HIS LOVE I
SEE

LOVE PURE AND SIMPLE AND IS HOW HER SPIRIT IS SO SWEET
SHE SIMPLY KNOWS NO BAD ONLY JOYFUL SPIRITUAL HAPPY
CHILD

STAY WITH ME FOREVER MY LOVE FOR YOU ARE MY MERCY GIRL
THE LORD BLESSED ME TRULY WHEN YOU CAME INTO MY
WORLD

ROSE PORTILLO

Pains Of The Heart

LOST IN THE DEPTHS OF THE TWELTHS OF NEVER
STOLEN BY THE DEVIL HIMSELF STRAIGHT INTO HELL
INCAPABLE OF FEELING ANY LOVE INSIDE ANY LONGER
CAPTURED NOT TO GIVE ANY RELIEF OR ANY HOPE EITHER

ANY OF THE PAIN FOUND THAT IS LYING DEEP WITHIN
SO MUCH OF IT DYING TRYING SOLELY TO SURVIVE
LITERALLY SITTING WITHIN FOLDS OF UNCOVERED LOVE
TRYING TO REACH THE TOPS OF SINKING LOVE'S RESIDUALS

ON A DAILY BASIS THEY ONLY PRETEND AND WANT TO PRY
BECOMING DEADLIER THAN ANY SOUL CAN KNOW OR ASK WHY
ONLY TO BECOME MORE COVERED YES DEEPER THAN BEFORE
AS EACH HURT AND EACH PAIN EVENTUALLY JUST PASSES BY

THE PAINS OF THE HEART ARE FOREVER BEING WOUNDED
MEMORIES OF THE UNFORGIVEN YET STILL ASKING WHY
THE UNKNOWN OF THE PRESENCE OF THE ILL FATED DEATH
THE IGNORANCE OF TOMORROW WAS WHAT REALLY WENT

ROSE PORTILLO

My Minu

BEFORE THE DAY CAME THAT SHE WAS BORN
I ALREADY WARMED HER SOUL INSIDE OF MY WOMB

BEAUTY I KNEW IN MY HEART THAT SHE WOULD BEHOLD
HOW I KNEW ONLY FROM GOD THAT COULD YET BE TOLD

WAS IT MY PERSONALITY OR MY MOOD DURING PREGNANCY
OR IS IT THAT I BECAME OF WHAT HER CHARACTER WOULD BE

ALL I KNOW IS THAT I LET NO ONE OR NOTHING BOTHER ME
NOT A THING WAS IMPORTANT AS TO SET ANY ANGER FREE

FROM WITHIN THE DEPTHS OF MY OWN HEART OF LOVE
I FELT THAT YES MY DAUGHTER WOULD BE THE ESSENCE OF

AND ON THE BEAUTIFUL WONDERFUL FOURTH OF JULY DAY
ON MY FATHER'S BIRTHDAY MAKING EVEN HIM EVER SO HAPPY

SO THE LOVING SPIRIT OF GOD GIVEN BEAUTIFUL LOVING SOUL
BECAME WHAT I HAD FELT ALL ALONG WITH MY LOVE UNTOLD

AND JUST TO MATCH AS THE YEARS MY LITTLE GIRL GREW
GOD TRULY BLESSED MY LIFE ALSO WITH THE WOMAN HE KNEW

SO MUCH ON THE INSIDE WAS HER WORLD FOR SHE STILL SHINES
OUTSTANDING WAS HER OUTER BEAUTY WITHIN GOD'S RIGHTS

ROSE PORTILLO

Eva Marie

AS I WAS TOLD SHE WAS MY LITTLE GIRL THAT DAY
I KNEW ALREADY MY LOVE FOR HER IT WAS MY WAY

IT WAS DIFFERENT FOR HER ALL ALONG EVEN THOUGH
THIS WAS TRUE IN HER EYES AND EVEN THEN I KNEW

SHE WAS QUIET YET STRONG MINDED OH THIS HAS BEEN TRUE
I WISH THERE WAS A WAY I COULD TELL HER THE TRUTH

SO MUCH HIDDEN ABOUT HIM SO MUCH SHE DOESN'T KNOW
NOT WANTING CHAOS HOPING WITH ME SHE'LL LOVE TO SOW

BUT TO KNOW THIS ABOUT HER SHE'S GOOD AND SWEET
MAYBE THIS IS WHY TO ME SHE WAS ALWAYS MY "COOKIE"

NOT FOR HER AND IT ALWAYS SEEMED THAT WAY TOO
BUT SHE WOULD TAKE OFF THE COAT ON HER BACK FOR YOU

IT'S OKAY THAT THE LOVE IN MY HEART SHE CAN'T SEE
I LOVE HER SO MUCH ONLY SHE JUST WON'T LET IT BE

WHEN THE DAY COMES AND I AM NO LONGER HERE
SOMEONE TELL HER I LOVE HER AND I WILL SEE HER THERE

ROSE PORTILLO

Angel Baby

BEAUTIFUL EBONY LOCKS OF CURLS GIVING THEM A WHIRL
I PRAYED FOR AS TRUE AS THE LORD I BORE A LITTLE GIRL

SHE WAS EVERY THING IN HER NAME THAT I WISHED FOR
AS A LITTLE GIRL STOOD SO PRETTY JUST AS A PEARL

WHEN EVERYONE SETS THEIR EYES ON HER BEAUTIFUL FACE
THE ONLY NAME WOULD FIT IS THOUGH ADORNED IN LACE

ANGEL'S HER NAME MY ANGEL GIRL YES I WANTED HER TO BE
I NAMED HER WHAT I FELT FROM HEAVEN FOR EVERYONE TO SEE

ALTHOUGH I KNOW SOMETHING ELSE WOULD HAVE TAKEN
PLACE
HER MIND HER HEART ALWAYS FULL OF LOVE NEVER GOING
ASTRAY

THE LOVE I HAVE ALWAYS FOR HER SHE HAS NEVER BEEN AWAY
HOW I WISH HER TO KNOW TO ME SHE'S ALWAYS JUST LIKE GOLD

KEEP HER IN YOUR ARMS CLOSE LORD JUST SO SHE COULD KNOW
HOLD ON TO HER TIGHT AND PLEASE GOD DON'T LET HER GO

IN CASE IF SHE MAY WANT TO CALL FOR ME AFTER I'M GONE
LET HER KNOW THAT I NEVER WANTED HER TO BE LEFT ALONE

ROSE PORTILLO

My Funny Face

AS I WOULD SING TO MY BEAUTY FOR I ALWAYS LOVE HER SO
FUNNY FACE I LOVE YOU YES SHE'D CRY NEVER LETTING GO

IF IT WAS MY WAY I'D TELL HER JUST HOW DEAR SHE WAS
WITH A SMILE AND A TUG I NEVER LET HER SHED A TEAR

FOR SHE HAD THE CUTEST FACE ON HER YOU EVER DID SEE
FUNNY FACE YOU ARE A BEAUTY YOU MEAN THE WORLD TO ME

I WOULD SAY THIS IS MY DARLENE MY DARLENE MY DARLENE
FOREVER I WILL CHERISH THOSE MOMENTS OF MY EVERY WORDS

ALL SHE EVER WANTED WAS FOR ME TO BE WITH HER ONLY
STILL TO THIS DAY SHE LOVES BEING AROUND ME SHE'S SO
SWEET

WITH ALL OF MY HEART MY LOVE IS FOR YOU ALWAYS MY
DARLENE
MY BEAUTY BABY GIRL FUNNY FACE FOR YOU I WILL ALWAYS BE

YOUR MOTHER LOVES YOU DARLENE WITH ALL OF HER HEART
DON'T EVER FORGET THAT BABY WHEN I LEAVE AND I DO PART

YOUR MOM,
ROSE

Cherie Amour

SHE WAS ALWAYS THE LIGHT OF MY EYES
SHE WAS MY SHINING STAR IN THE NIGHT

A WONDERFUL BABY SO SWEET AND SO LOVING
SO JOYFULLY INTO HER BEAUTIFUL BABY BUTTON SELF

SHE WAS MY BOOGIE MY CHERIE AMOUR MY CUTIE PIE
WHEN I ASKED HER NAME SHE'D SAY CHERIE AMOUR SO BRIGHT

SHE'D SIMPLY AS A MATTER OF FACTLY ALWAYS JUST SAY
SMILING HER SMILE AND ANSWER CHERIE AMOUR OF COURSE!

MY SWEET DARLING IS WHAT MY BABY GIRL'S NAME MEANS
SHE HOLDS TRUE TO HER NAME PLEASE ALWAYS TO HER BE
SWEET

I LOVED HER IN MY WOMB FEELING HER SO TINY AND SO SMALL
EVEN IN HER TINY LOVING CRY I COULD FEEL HER NEED FOR
LOVE

I LOVED HER THEN AND I'LL MISS MY BABY I STILL LOVE HER
NOW
AS I LOOK IN HER PRETTY EYES HER LOVE FOR ME THEY DO TELL

HER LOVE IN HER HEART HER NEED FOR LOVE SO ME SHE CALLS
DEAR LORD PLEASE TAKE CARE OF HER FOR SHE'S MY BABY MY
DOLL

FOR MY ROSE,
YOUR MOM;
ROSE PORTILLO

"Brilliance Is His Name"

MY FIRST BORN SON BRILLIANCE IS HIS NAME
SO MUCH A PART OF MY HEART LET HIM KNOW HE STILL IS

SO HARD TO UNDERSTAND HIS TOUGHTS AND HIS MIND
MY FAULT HIS ANGER FOR I CRIED SO MUCH BEFORE HE CAME

TRYING HARD WITH ALWAYS A MAN TO MAKE HIM BE
FORGETTING MY LOVE INSTEAD WAS JUST FOR HIM TO SEE

WILL FOREVER ALWAYS ASK HIS PARDON AND FORGIVENESS
FOR NOT GIVING HIM ALL MY HUGS AND ALL OF MY KISSES

I'M SORRY BUT NOT FOR WHAT ALL THAT HE HAS BECOME
A BEAUTIFUL INTELLIGENT LOVING GOOD HEARTED MAN

ALL THE TREATMENT I THOUGHT WAS GOOD WAS TOO HARD
WHAT I COULD HAVE SHOULD HAVE IS OVER AND DONE!

I MISS HIM HE'S LOST SOMEWHERE OUT THERE IT SEEMS
PLEASE GOD FIND MY SON AND TELL HIM TO COME HOME!

LET HIM KNOW THAT THERE IS NO WHERE ELSE HE SHOULD BE
ME AND HIS CHILDREN MISS HIM SO MUCH AND ITS US HE NEEDS

LITTLE DOES HE KNOW THAT I'M SORRY FOR ALL THE WHAT
NOTS
WHAT I COULD DO TO MAKE UP FOR BEING SO HARD IT'S ME HIS
MOM

LORD GOD HELP ME GET MY SON BACK HOME TO YOUR LAND!
I NEED HIM BY MY SIDE IF HE DOES NOT RETURN TO US I WILL
DIE

YOU ARE THE VERY MEANING OF YOUR NAME MY LOVE MY SON
YOU'RE TRULY THE FIRST MAN OF MY HEART AND SOUL MY SONG

BORN OF MY FLESH MY LOVE MY VERY BEING AND ALL MY PAIN
YOU THE FIRST MAN OF MY BLOOD ALL I WANTED WAS FOR YOUR
GAIN

TO JAVIER, YOUR MOM

Her

THE DAY I FIRST SAW HER STANDING THERE ALL ALONE
SMILING AT THE SIGHT OF HER AS SHE SHYLY LOOKED AWAY
AND AS I TURNED TO FOLLOW HER ONLY TO FIND A SHADOW
I COULD ALWAYS ONLY FEEL HER SADNESS AND UNCERTAINTY

SO PRETTY YET SO MUCH SADNESS ME FOREVER ASKING WHY
WHAT IS IT THAT MADE HER BECOME IN A MELANCHOLIC WAY
SOMEONE HURT HER WHEN SO YOUNG VERY BAD SO I ASK WHY
THE DEEP SIGHING COMES FROM WITHIN THE LONGING INSIDE

SHE PASSED ME BY EACH DAY I WANTED HER SO MUCH TO HOLD
I STILL SEARCH FOR HER HAIR HER EYES HER I FIND BUT NO
SMILE
ANYTHING ANY SIGN FROM HER BACK THEN I THOUGHT I WILL
DO
I FOUND MYSELF CRAVING FOR HER INSIDE MY HEART ALL THE
WHILE

EVEN HER FROWN FROM HER WAS A BEAUTIFUL SIGHT TO SEE
FINALLY ONCE OUR EYES DID MEET THEN SHE SMILED ONLY FOR
ME
AS IF SHE WERE TO BE ANGRY AT ME HER HAUNTING EYES
DARED
STARING BACK I KNEW TO BE FOR A WONDER MIRACLE IT
SEEMED

THEN GIGGLING AS A LITTLE GIRL AS I SAW HER LAUGHING IN
GLEE
NEVER HAD LOVE FELT SO AMAZINGLY DEEP INSIDE FOR ME TO
BE SO HAPPY
YES I KNEW IN MY HEART SHE KNEW HOW I FELT ABOUT HER ALL
ALONG
WE BOTH KNEW WHEN OUR EYES MET AGAIN SHE WAS
SEARCHING FOR ME!

I WAS ALREADY IN LOVE WITH HER I KNEW THIS RIGHT FROM
THE START
HER LOVE I COULD FEEL HER LONELINESS LINGERED STILL NOT
LEAVING
WHAT WORLD WAS SHE IN BEFORE TODAY TO MAKE HER FEEL SO
VERY SAD?
WHO WAS IN HER LIFE WHO HURT HER WHO SADDENED HER
HEART SO BAD?

WHAT KEPT HER FROM GIVING ME ALL OF HER LOVE INSIDE OF
HER SOUL
WHAT WAS IT I NEEDED TO DO I DIDN'T GET TO DO I WAS LOSING
CONTROL
WHY DIDN'T SHE TELL ME WHAT IT WAS THAT I KNEW WAS
GOING WRONG
I CAN'T HELP HER NOW FOR I LEFT HER WORLD AND MY SOUL
NOW IS GONE!

TONY

Tony, My Son

HIS NAME AFTER MY FIRST LOVE HE IS THE LIGHT OF MY EYES
ALWAYS HANDLING IT ALL FOR ME NOT TO BARE ANY HARM
NEVER WANTING ME TO BE HURT BY ANYONE ANY MORE
LIKE THE ONE I LOVE HIS STRENGTH HE GAVE TO YOU MY ONE

YOU WERE BORN TO WATCH OVER ME THIS TRULY WHAT I
BELIEVE
LOVING YOU FROM WITHIN THE SECRETS OF THE DEPTH OF MY
SOUL
YOU HELD THE KEY TO THE DOOR THE WINDOWS OF MY HEART
AS HE
STAY WHO YOU HAVE ALWAYS BEEN FOR ME THAT IS WHO YOU
ARE

HELPING THE MEMORY OF THE KING OF MY HEART AND HIS
TRUE LOVE
EVEN AS HE GLANCED INTO YOUR EYES HIM KNOWING IT WAS
YOU
HIS SMILE OF APPROVAL OF ALL THAT YOU WERE SO LITTLE SO
GOOD
REMINDING HIM OF HIMSELF PROUD OF YOU BEING SENT FROM
ABOVE

YOUR LOVE FOR ME CONSTANTLY GIVES ME THE FAITH I
THOUGHT I LOST
IN KNOWING THAT YOU CARRY WITH SO MUCH GRACE AND
NOBLENESS
THE LOVE FOR ME THE CARE YOU TAKE AS HE WOULD ALWAYS
WANT
BLESSED I AM FOR YOU IN MY LIFE TONY YOU ARE TRULY THE
ONE

I LOVE YOU TONY
YOUR MOM

I Feel Your Warmth

I FEEL YOUR WARMTH
AS I MOVE HERE ALL ABOUT

I REMEMBER YOUR TOUCH
OF YOUR HAND HOLDING MINE

I FEEL YOU STRIDE BESIDE ME
AS I WALK UNDER THE SUN

YOU ARE MY ONLY COMFORT
IN THE DARKNESS OF THE NIGHT

I STILL TASTE YOUR KISSES
AS I SIT STILL TO REMINISCE WITH

I CAN HEAR YOUR LAUGHTER
WHEN YOUR EYES MET MINE

ALTHOUGH DAYS OF OUR LOVE
ARE GONE STILL ENDLESSLY NOT

RECALLING OUR LONG STILL NIGHTS
FOREVER FEELING US BEING TORN APART

YOU ARE HERE IN THE AIR AS I SPEAK
YOUR BREATH I HEAR AS I SLEEP

YOUR LIPS NEVER DRYING MY TEARS
AS BEING SHED EACH NIGHT BREAKS

WATCHING YOUR SMILES IN MY MIND
UPON MY PILLOW EACH NIGHT AS I FIND

ROSE PORTILLO

Believing In Yourself

BELIEVING IN YOURSELF IS THE POWER
WHATEVER YOU THINK YOU ARE YOU WILL BE

DO NOT UNDERESTIMATE YOUR TRUE VALUE
FOR YOU WILL BE WHATEVER YOU BELIEVE

CHARACTER IS GETTING UP AFTER EVERY SLIP AND FALL
TO SEARCH FOR THE WILDFLOWERS LEFT IN THE ROCKS

IF YOU ACCEPT THE UNHAPPINESS IN YOUR LIFE
YOU WILL BE UNHAPPY AND EXACTLY WHAT YOU ACCEPT

DO NOT FORGET THAT TO FOREVER DANCE ALONG THE WAY
AND REMEMBER WHAT YOU SEND YOU WILL ALWAYS RECEIVE

NEVER DOUBT YOURSELF IN THE DARKNESS OR IN LIGHT
JUST BECAUSE YOU DO NOT SEE DOESN'T MEAN IT WILL NOT
SHINE

FOR THE LORD GOD GIVES US THE MOST RADIANT LIGHT
SO THAT WE MAY SEE ALL THAT IS NOT SHOWN FROM ABOVE

LOVE YOURSELF AND LIVE WITH YOUR CONSCIENCE GOOD
WISDOM IN YOUR SOUL WILL SHOW THROUGH SINGING LOVE

YOUR SPIRIT IS EVER CHANGING WITH THE GOD'S LOVE INSIDE
EVER LASTING LIGHT GOD GIVES US TO FOREVER ALWAYS DANCE

ROSE

This One's To You Mom

You think you know me inside and out
But now let me tell you what it's about

How you make me feel
And secrets I have concealed

Deep inside my very core
Where about I am very unsure

I love you but I really don't like you
You could probably say the same about me too

Some day I wish I could just run away
Kinda like uh . . . today cuz today I can't stand you

Or your dumb remarks
I feel like now I'm in disregard

To everything that is all around me
Gosh! I can't wait til I'm eighteen

What am I here for besides favors
I feel deprived to taste all of life's flavors

Because of you I have no friends
And to everyone else I have to pretend

That I'm happy in this mental state
Of being sad and of being afraid

Of the real world and of life, Mom!
You're pushing me closer to that knife

If I weren't here the only difference
Would be that there is more dirty dishes

I feel trapped against my will
I'll be stuck here until

My sanity is gone
Then it will be me whose wrong . . .

When it was really YOU!

Annonymously Written
. . . for So Pretty So Many Tears

Thank You God

THANK YOU GOD FOR THE SKY I LOOK ABOVE
THAT STAYS ABOVE US AS WE ALL CAN BREATH

THANK YOU FOR ALL THE PRECIOUS TIME GIVEN
YES I STILL HAVE MY FAMILY WITH LOVE IN US

THANK YOU FOR THE OCEAN STILL AROUND SO LONG
HOLDING PRECIOUS WATER AND IT'S LIFE AMONG

THANK YOU GOD FOR ALL MY BLESSED CHILDREN
LET'S NOT WASTE TIME BY NOT SEEING THEM TODAY

THANK YOU FOR STILL KEEPING ME ALIVE AND RIGHT
TO BE ABLE TO SAY HELLO AND TO SAY GOODBYE

THANK YOU GOD EVEN THOUGH I FEEL SO ALONE
I MUST REMEMBER AS LONG AS I HAVE YOU IT'S TRUE

THANK YOU GOD FOR SENDING ME HERE ON EARTH
IN ALL THAT I SEE AND HEAR FROM YOU I LEARN

THANK YOU GOD FOR THE FUN AND JOY WE CAN HAVE
NO ONE REALLY APPRECIATES UNTIL IT'S TOO LATE

THANK YOU GOD FOR ALL THE FRIENDLY SINCERE SMILES
THAT HUNGER IN RETURN ALONG THE LONELY WHILES

THANK YOU GOD FOR THE GOOD PEOPLE THAT ARE LEFT
AS TIME GOES BY THINKING THAT THEY'RE ALL DEAD

THANK YOU FOR TEACHING ME FROM YOU ARE THE SMILES
TO COUNT MY BLESSINGS IN ALL AND EVERYTHING I DO

THANK YOU FOR I CAN SEE BEAUTY IN THIS UGLY WORLD
HOPING NO ONE DESTROYS WHAT YOU BLESSED US WITH

THANK YOU GOD FOR ANYTHING I MAY HAVE IGNORED
IT'S TRUE I SUFFERED SO LONG UNTIL I'VE BEEN BURNED

THANK YOU GOD FOR KNOWING THAT MY DAYS ARE NUMBERED
SO THRIFT ARE THEY MERELY A BLINK OF ANY EYE UNTURNED

WHAT WILL BECOME OF ME MY SPIRIT MY SOUL DO YOU SEE
SIMPLE DEEPNESS LYING AHEAD OR IS IT HEAVEN FOR ME?

ROSE PORTILLO

I Told You

I TOLD YOU THERE WOULD NEVER BE ANYONE FOR ME LIKE YOU
WHY DID YOU LEAVE MY WORLD AND WHY WAS I SUCH A FOOL
WHY DID YOU BELIEVE HER WHEN SHE SAID I LEFT YOU ALONE
WHY DIDN'T YOU FIGHT HARDER FOR YOU I WAS COMING HOME

YOU TOLD ME YOU WANTED ME TO BE HAPPY AND TO FIND LOVE
ALL THOSE NIGHTS I CRIED KNOWING YOU WERE GOING TO DIE
YOU LEFT ME COLD ALONE WHEN YOU PASSED AWAY THAT DAY
I WAS COMING BACK YOU COULD'VE WAITED A LITTLE LONGER

I NEVER WANTED ANY OTHER MAN I CAN NEVER LOVE ANY
OTHER
DIDN'T YOU BELIEVE ME WHEN I SAID I COULDN'T LIVE
WITHOUT YOU
SO YOUR PRESENCE LINGERS ON HERE IN MY MIND AND MY SOUL
YOU SAID YOU WOULD COME BACK TO FIND ME WHEREVER I'D
GO?

IT'S BEEN 25 YEARS SINCE YOU LEFT MY WORLD MY SIDE MY LIFE
YOU ARE MY LOVE THERE ARE NO TOMORROWS FOR ME
ANYMORE
NOT WITHOUT THE ONE THAT STILL RESIDES IN EVERY BREATH I
TAKE
I AM NOT HAPPY HERE I'M LOST EVERY MINUTE EVERY DAY I JUST
CRY

IT'S HORRIBLE TORMENT IT'S CRUEL AND UNUSUAL
PUNISHMENT
FOR I AM LEFT IN THIS WORLD TO FIGHT OFF THE UGLY EVIL
DEMONS
I TOLD YOU THAT THEY WERE GOING TO HURT ME AND BE SO
MEAN
THERE IS NOT AND NEVER WILL BE ANYONE THAT LOVES ME
YOUR WAY

THERE WILL NEVER BE ANOTHER LOVE LIKE WHAT I HAD WITH
YOU
NO ONE COMPARES TO YOU OR YOUR LOVE THAT YOU GAVE TO
ME
WITHOUT YOU I DON'T WANT TO LIVE AND ALL I WANT TO DO IS
DIE
WHEN ARE YOU COMING BACK TO ME TO SEE THE LOVE I HAVE
FOR YOU?

I AM WAITING FOR YOU STILL AS I TOLD YOU FOREVER AND A DAY
BUT YOU TOLD ME FOREVER AND ETERNITY THAT YOUR LOVE
FOR ME
WHERE THEN DID YOU GO WHY DID YOU TAKE YOUR LOVE AWAY?
HAVE YOU FOUND YOUR SHINING STAR UP IN THAT LONELY SKY I
SEE

FOR THERE MAY BE A MILLION STARS THAT COME OUT EACH
NIGHT
AS I LOOK UP AND AS I GO SEARCHING FOR ONLY YOUR LIGHTED
SOUL
I SEE NOTHING NO SHINING STAR FOR ME AS I WAIT EACH NIGHT
I DIE
FOR THERE IS NOTHING BUT LONELINESS IN THESE LONELY DAYS
I FIND

EVEN WITH ALL THE PEOPLE IN THE WORLD THERE IS NOBODY
LEFT HERE
IT'S OVER TO SOME THAT YOU ARE JUST GONE BUT MY HEART
LINGERS ON
AS I GO TO SEARCH THE WORLD OVER AS YOU SAID YOU WOULD
DO TOO
I CAN'T SEE FOR THERE IS NO ONE THERE FOR ME I JUST CAN'T
FIND YOU

I ASKED YOU NOT TO EVER LEAVE TO FOREVER STAY AND BE BY
MY SIDE
THERE IS NOBODY TO TAKE CARE OF ME OR NO ONE TO EVER
LOVE ME
I TOLD YOU THAT I WOULD NEVER LOVE ANYONE THE WAY I
LOVED YOU
YOU INSISTED TO FIND SOMEONE ELSE TO MAKE ME LOVE ALL
OVER AGAIN

TAKE ME WITH YOU WHEREVER YOU ARE I CAN'T BE HERE ANY
LONGER
I TOLD YOU THAT WITHOUT YOUR LOVE IN MY LIFE I WOULDN'T
SURVIVE
I WANTED TO DIE WITH YOU WHEN I SAW YOU IN THE COFFIN
LYING THERE
PRAYING YOU PLEASE TAKE ME I DON'T WANT TO DIE WITHOUT
YOU STILL

ROSE PORTILLO

Leave Me Alone

LEAVE ME ALONE NOW THIS I PLEA
ALL I'VE EVER WANTED IS JUST TO BE FREE

YOU'VE HAD YOUR FUN AND ALL THE TEASING
LET IT BE DONE WITH ALL YOUR POKING AT ME

I'VE BEEN HURT ALL THIS TIME ARE YOU HAPPY
TEARS ARE HERE STILL YES THEY'LL FOREVER BE

YOU CAN CAUSE ALL THE PAIN AND SADNESS TOO
THE ONE THING YOU DO NOT KNOW I WILL STAY TRUE

A DAMAGED HEART TEAR STAINED SOUL HERE TO STAY
YOU WOULDN'T STOP AT ANYTHING UNTIL IT'S YOUR WAY

NOW I'M GROWING OLD AND THE PRETTY FACE IS GONE
ALL MY WRINKLES SHOW HARD FROM ALL THAT WENT WRONG

INSTEAD OF TRYING TO TAKE IT TO THE END OF ME
LEAVE ME ALONE NOW PLEASE THIS FOREVER I WILL PLEA

I NEVER HURT YOU I DON'T KNOW WHY YOU HATE ME
I'LL NEVER UNDERSTAND WHY PEOPLE ARE SO MEAN

WHEN I'M GONE BECAUSE THIS WORLD WAS SO HATEFUL
PLEASE REMEMBER ONE THING ABOUT ME I NEVER HATED YOU

NONE OF YOU EVEN THOSE THAT WANTED MY HURT SO BAD
I ALWAYS HELPED I TOOK YOU UNDER MY WING TOO SAD

ROSE PORTILLO

Truth

SOMETIMES WE DO NOT WANT TO SEE THE TRUTH
MAYBE UNKNOWINGLY WE DO WANT TO SEE WHAT IS TRUE

BUT THEN WE SUDDENLY FIND OUT TRUTH HAS IT'S WAY
OF FINDING OUT WHERE WE ARE BY LIVING LIFE ALL ALONE

MISTAKES SO GREAT CAN BE SO HARD TO LIVE THROUGH
WE MUST LEAVE OUR MISTAKES LET THEM GO IN THE WIND

ONLY TO FIND THE TRUTH WAITING FOR US ALL ALONG
WHILE WE WERE RUNNING TRYING TO HIDE FROM THE TRUTH

NOT KNOWING THAT LIFE HAS A WAY OF TELLING US THE TRUTH
WITH THE WIND IT TELLS US BY HITTING US RIGHT IN OUR FACE

YES SOMETIMES WHEN WE TRY TO RUN FROM THE TRUTH
WHEN WE LIE TO OURSELVES AND OTHERS TRYING TO PRETEND

WE WILL SOMETIMES TRY TO CHANGE THE TRUTH TO OTHERS
AGAIN COMING WITH A BREEZE IT WILL HIT US RIGHT IN THE FACE

SOME CALL IT KARMA SOME CALL IT WILL HARD AS IT IS TO
PLACE
WHAT GOES AROUND ALWAYS COMES BACK AROUND RIGHT TO
US

EVEN IF AS HARD AS WE TRY TO MAKE IT SO UNREAL IN LIFE
AS MUCH AS WE DON'T LIKE IT AS MUCH AS IT WILL DEFINITELY
BE

TRUTH AS IT'S OWN WAY OF KNOWING WHEN TO COME TOO
RIGHT WHEN WE THINK THAT ALL THAT WE LIED ABOUT IS
GONE

THERE IT IS HERE IT IS IN FRONT OF OUR FACE NOT MISSING
ANYTHING
AS WE LAUGH THINKING ALL IS HAPPY AS WE ALL BEGIN TO SING

HERE SHE COMES LAUGHING RIGHT ALONG WITH YOU AND ME
MISS TRUTH AS WE WISH A WOMAN TO BE SHE HEARS US AND
SEES

BET YOUR DOLLARS WITH ME YES SHE WILL COME TO YOU SO
FREE
AND TELL YOU ALL ABOUT IT WITH ALL THE OTHERS THERE TO
OBSERVE

ALWAYS AS FREE AS A DOVE AND LOVING IN THE SKY AS A BIRD
THE TRUTH WILL COME TELL EVERYONE YES SHE WILL SET YOU
FREE

ROSE PORTILLO

His Marriage

THE VOWS THAT WERE MADE ON THE DAY OF HIS WED
ALREADY WERE ULTERIOR MOTIVES ALL UP IN HIS HEAD

IT SEEMED AS IF HE KNEW RIGHT FROM THE START
WHAT HIS AWFUL ACTIONS WERE BEING DONE FOR

OF ALL THE HURT HE HELD BACK FROM *HIS* PAST
IT WAS AS IF IT TO HURT ME WAS HIS CHOICE OF ART

NOT REALLY CARING ABOUT ANYONE BUT HIMSELF
THE HARDNESS INSIDE HIS HEART KNOWING WE'D PART

I FELT I COULD SAVE HIM THOUGH FROM ALL HIS PAIN
SO SCARED INSIDE OF ME WHEN HIS MEANNESS CAME

ONCE WE WERE MARRIED ALL I EVER DID WAS CRY
ACCEPTING THE FACT HE LOVED ME OR THAT HE DID NOT

LEAVING MY OWN HURTS FROM BEING SO BADLY ABUSED
YOU'D THINK WITH HIS SOUL ALL THAT WOULD BE THOUGH

BEING HONEST WITH HIM JUST CAUSED HIM TO HATE MORE
THROWING EVERYTHING I TOLD HIM ALL THE TIME AT MY FACE

NOW HE'S GONE WITH MY BROKEN SPIRIT LEAVING HEARTACHES
AND HERE I AM ALL ALONE HE LEFT ME WENT WITH MY FRIEND

HAD I FOLLOWED MY INSTINCTS I WOULD HAVE KNOWN BACK
THEN
THE SIGNS WERE THERE AT HIS MARRIAGE WORDS WRITTEN IN
BOLD

ROSE PORTILLO

Deadly Alcohol

THE DRINKING OF WHAT IS THIS DEADLY ALCOHOL
DEBILITATING ANY BEAUTY FROM THE NOBLEST OF SOULS

SO EVIL IT IS BY HOW EASY IT BEGINS IT'S UGLY TORMENT
SO DEADLY AFTER WHAT IS LEFT OF ANY SORT OF HUMAN BEING

BRUTALIZING AND DIRTYING THE CLEANEST OF ALL MINDS
TAKING ALL GOOD AWAY FROM THE PUREST OF ALL HEARTS

FINALLY RETURNING BRINGING ALL MANKIND TO INSANITY
PUTTING IN THOUGHTS OF SO MANY DIFFERENT FILTHY
IMPURITIES

SURGING THE BRAINS DROWNING WITH SUCH DEADLY ALCOHOL
BY MISTREATING THEIR MOST CHERISHED OF ALL LOVED ONES

FILLING THEIR LIVES WITH SO MANY FALSE ADORATIONS AND
LIES
BY THE WAY OF FALSE ILLUSIONS AND THE SICK EVILNESS INSIDE

DRAINING ANY INTELLIGENCE AND LOVE ONE ONCE HELD
WITHIN
CONFUSING US WITH WHAT ONCE WAS AND ALL THE REASONS
WHY

SADNESS OF WHAT THIS DEADLY ALCOHOL DOES TO MAKE US
BLEED
DYING WITH NO ONE LEFT BELIEVING IN TEARS BEGGING
TRYING TO RETURN

HOW THIS DEADLY VENOM ALCOHOL CAN CHANGE US INTO
SOMEONE ELSE
BY THE WAY OF CAUSING CRUEL TREATMENT AND MEANNESS TO
ALL

BEGINNING WITH FALSE GLAMOUR EASY PRETENSE HAVING SO
MUCH FUN
LEADING TO THE ROAD OF LONELINESS AND MOCKERY UNTIL
IT'S DONE

ROSE PORTILLO

Don't Be Sad

DON'T BE SAD
NOW IT TIME FOR ME TO GO

DON'T BE SAD

I'LL BE RIGHT HERE NEXT TO YOU
PUT YOUR HAND ON YOUR HEART

THAT'S WERE I AM

SO DON'T BE SAD

I'LL VISIT YOU SOON
NO MATTER WHAT WAIT

DON'T BE SAD

I'LL ALWAYS BE HERE NEXT TO YOU
SOMEBODY'S WITH YOU

IF YOUR SAD
JUST HUG WHOS WITH YOU

DON'T BE SAD

I'LL ALWAS BE
RIGHT THERE IN YOUR HEART

NOW TAKE MY HAND
AND SAY GOODBYE

**FROM
LENA GODINEZ**

**TO HER DADDY
8 YEARS OLD**

No Response

FINALLY NO RESPONSE REGARDING LOVING HIM
NO ENTHUSIASM TOWARD US BEING TOGETHER
JUST THE WAY HE ACTED AS THOUGH HE NEVER WAS
VENGEANCE NO - IT'S BEEN ENOUGH - MUCH HATRED

FORGIVENESS OKAY BUT WHY SO MUCH SADNESS
DEEP SADNESS MELANCHOLIC DEPRESSION STILL
JUST SMALL SMILES ONLY AT TIMES THAT SEEP OUT
THOUGHTLESS MOMENTS BETWEEN OUR TIMES ALONE

WONDERING WHY THINGS WENT THE WAY THEY GO
TO SEE IF MAYBE THERE IS ANY LOVE BETWEEN US
IF THERE WAS EVER ANY LOVE THERE ASIDE OUR SONGS
SOMBERNESS ALWAYS EVEN INSIDE OUR HIDDEN LAUGHTER

ALLOWING HIM TO SEE ALL THE SADNESS HE NEVER KNEW
FROM SUCH A LONG LONG TIME AGO THAT HE TRIED TO SEW
NO WORDS REALLY WERE SPOKEN EVER AGAIN ABOUT IT
ONLY LOVE UNSPOKEN AND INSINCERITY SHOWN UNSAID

GOING A LONG WAY JUST TO ALWAYS SHOW SO JUST A LITTLE
WHAT WAS LYING JUST BENEATH AND UNDER OUR SOULS
THE HAPPINESS AND FUN DAYS WE REALLY THOUGHT WE HAD
BEING HIDDEN NOW FOREVER MORE KNOWING EVEN SO

NEVER TO SHOW MY TRUE FEELINGS NOT TO HIM EVER AGAIN
WHAT WAS SO FREELY GIVEN FROM MY HEART DEEP WITHIN
NOW WITHHELD ALWAYS WILL BE YES EVEN FOREVER IN THE
END
TO EXPRESS THE UNFORBIDDEN THE HURT AND ALL THE PAIN

ROSE PORTILLO

My Heart Breaks

With the dawn my heart breaks into little pieces
As I sit in some lonely dark room with fright
Feeling so lost alone without a friend in sight
Why do I wait for you so deep amongst the past

How did I lose the only one that meant anything
The only one in my life that treated me so right
All the others hating me are still here very much alive
I wait forever in the eye of the storm for you so alone

Lost in the storm that grows strong how I wish I was home
Strangely visioning looking through until all else is gone
Tears in my eyes hurting blurring and straining my view
Lost forever I can't be found it hurts so bad with you gone

It's chaos inside the hell of it waiting for the storm to stop
Hating their filthy lies as their ugliness rises to finally show
Hatred so evil so monstrous and fierce how can anyone fight
Lord God all I ask is with him I plead to take me home now

Rose Portillo

When I Was A Little Girl

Back when I was a little girl I always wanted to "go home,"
I knew there was going to be nothing but pain here for me.
Praying all those nights for God to save me from this hell,
This place had all the evil from some place I had known once.

Crying each day to leave this hell especially alone late at night,
To God I'd ask to take me back home and from this ugly world.
The evil that lurked here here for me was so horrible and cruel,
Not just a feeling I had it was from an old prophecy turned true.

Somehow at seven I knew at twenty seven I was going to die,
He died at twenty seven instead but it was I too, who lost my life.
"*My First Love*" left my world and I thought the coffin was for me,
The evil predicted from then was always there waiting to be set free

Now at I'm fifty with him gone all I feared to happen has come along,
Everything was cursed and his death destined for my life to be wrong.
All "*True Hearts*" having love for only me have left this world too,
No one to love me living here in this world only those who are not true.

Strange enough, though everything I had declared within became reality,
Since I had not spoken from my lips maybe somehow I release the force.
This horrible evil occurred and since I beg finally for only God's peace,
Remembering the evil to come with fear to stay now with fear not to leave.

Rose Portillo

The Day I Died

That day I died was all of a peaceful loving
Never had I ever felt such a wonderful feeling
All noise around ended yes the silence was golden
I tried to tell them all not to worry for I was okay

I saw everything and everyone it was all so clear
So vivid the visions that still stay in my head
The peace was so awesome I didn't want to wake
Pleading thinking they could hear what I had said

I felt they could see me thinking my eyes were open
Assuming they knew to leave me be saying I was okay
Only they were scared as they saw my body just laying
Running to where I was laying I reassured them to stay

But my mouth wouldn't open there was nothing I could say
Yet I could hear myself out loud saying the words that day
They ran as if they couldn't hear me saying for my body to leave
When they reached my body they all tried to wake me

Disturbing me with confusion set in for I thought I was alive
Telling them to leave me alone for there I truly wanted to stay
The longing to stay where I was laying in the quietness inside
My craving to stay alone where with peaceful silence became

As they touched me I began to hear them call my name,
"Are you okay? What happened, Oh My God! What happened?
So serene I felt, "Please leave me alone please let me stay."
But they took me away from the Golden Silence that I lay

Now that it is all passed I realize that The Lord wanted me to see,
That there is nothing to fear when you're ready to leave this world.
Death is a wonderful beautiful feeling with a peaceful golden silence,
So I see as I leave I will be happy with no regret knowing no fear at all.

Rose Portillo

245

Loving Death

LOVING DEATH FOR IT IS SO MUCH MORE SWEETER THAN LIFE
AS YOUR SOUL IS ENTWINED WITH ITS TIGHTENING CARESS

IT'S HAUNTING IT'S TAUNTING SWELLING DEEPENING URGE
THE ENTICING SLEEP OF LOVING DEATH ALL TOO SOON ARRIVES

THOUGH WITH ALL YOUR MIGHT YOU STILL NEED TO SUCCOMB
TO THE HEAVY SEDUCING FEELING UPON WHICH DEATH LIES

THE FEAR THAT ONCE RULED YOUR LIFE SUDDENLY IS GONE
FOR IT'S PEACEFUL CRAVING OVERRULING ALL THAT IS ALIVE

SUCH SWEETNESS THIS FEELING LOVING DEATH IS TRULY
STRANGE
DRAWING MY LIFE INTO EACH SECOND SURRENDER CHERISHED

THE LOVE OF DEATH BRINGS ONLY PEACE NOW SURRENDERING
INVITING ALWAYS ALLOWING IT TO SURVIVE INSIDE FOREVER

TO SLEEP THE FRIGHTFUL SLEEP IS NO LONGER AFRAID TO FIGHT
FINALLY HAVING THE PEACEFUL LOVING DEATH ONCE FULL OF
LIFE

INESCAPABLE UNAVOIDABLE IRRESISTABLE DEPTHS YOU DO
BELONG
PULLING YOU IN REELING YOU INSIDE DEEP INTO DEATHS
REALMS

WHERE DOES ALL OUR DESTINATION END WITH THE NEVER
LANDS
OF IT'S UNKNOWN REIGNS BEGINNING AND ONLY STAYING
AGAIN

ROSE PORTILLO

Love

LOVE CANNOT BE COMMANDED TO EAGERLY EXIST
LOVE SIMPLY IS WITHOUT SAYING IT JUST LIVES

LOVE CANNOT BE CONTROLLED BY ANYONE BEING BOLD
LOVE COMES FROM WITHIN OUR HEARTS OF GOLD

LOVE JUST SEEMS TO COME IT IS NATURALLY TO BE
LOVE ALSO CANNOT BE DEMANDED TO BE SO

LOVE SEEMS TO BE NEEDED BY US SO UNSELFISHLY
LOVE DOESN'T COME TO BE MADE OR FORCED TO BE

LOVE IS SOMEHOW FORMED INSIDE OF OUR SOULS
LOVE IS ALSO SO VERY MUCH INDEED UNCONTROLLABLE

WE ALSO CANNOT TELL OURSELVES WHO TO LOVE
WE CANNOT MAKE OUR HEARTS FALL OUT OF LOVE'S SPELL

WHEN LOVE IS REAL IT SIMPLY CANNOT BE UNDONE
IT IS PUT IN OUR HEARTS AND SOULS FOREVER UNSUNG

AND NO AMOUNT OF TIME AWAY CAN MAKE LOVE FADE
NO AMOUNT OF TIME TOGETHER CAN MAKE LOVE STAY

LOVE SIMPLY DECIDES TO ARRIVE ANY TIME ANY PLACE
TRUE LOVE WILL NEVER DIE OR CHANGE OR GO AWAY

REAL FOREVER LOVE NO MATTER WHAT WILL ALWAYS BE
FOREVER THROUGH THE END OF TIME TRUE LOVE IS ETERNITY!

ROSE PORTILLO

My Silent Killer

INSIDE OF EVERY CELL OF MY PAINFUL ACHING ONCE WELL BODY
LIVING DEEPER THAN FROM INSIDE WHERE MY BLOOD RUNS

THE BURNING STINGING AND HURTING OF INSIDE OF MY BONES
DIFFERENT TYPES OF PAIN ALL AT ONCE EVERYWHERE IT GOES

FIGHTING AGAINST ITSELF EACH WAKING MOMENT OF THE DAY
WHY MY BODY STAYS ALIVE IN THIS PAIN TO ME IS UNKNOWN

WAITING FOR THE DEATH OF IT THAT IT SURELY WILL BRING
WITH NO ONE WINNING IN THIS SICK CRUEL PAINFUL GAME

FOR THE WINNER IS THE LOSER INSIDE OF THE KILLER PAIN
WITH IT'S THROBBING CRUSHING INTO EACH MUSCLE STRAINED

AS IN RETALIATION THINKING OF PROTECTING IT'S OWN SICK
VIRUS
FEELING AS IF PUNCHING BAGS BEATING INSIDE WITH ALL IT'S
MIGHT

AS IF ALL MY SKIN HAS RAW LAYERS BURNING WITH EACH TOUCH
BUT PRAYING AND HOPING AS THE TEARS RUSH DOWN THE
NIGHTS

NOT OKAY THOUGH WAITING FOR IT TO SLOW DOWN AND GO
AWAY
MY SILENT KILLER IS SO AWFUL STILL I'M PRETENDING IT WON'T
STAY

ROSE PORTILLO

No More Pretending

ALL OF MY LIFE SINCE I WAS VERY YOUNG
THOSE DAYS PRETENDING IS ALL I'VE EVER DONE

I'VE PRETENDED LIFE WAS NOT SAD YOU WEREN'T GONE
I'VE TRIED HARD GAVE LIFE A CHANCE TO TRY TO BE MORE

I'VE PRETENDED TOO THAT PEOPLE WERE GOOD
I NEVER WANTED TO BELIEVE THAT SO MANY ARE BAD

INSIDE OF EVERYONE THERE IS A MEAN COLDNESS IT SEEMS
BUT I'VE PRETENDED SO LONG NOW I'M TIRED OF IT ALL

IT'S TIME FOR ME TO SHOW THE REAL FACE I HAVE ON
LIFE IS SHORT NOTHING IN THIS WORLD REALLY MATTERS

EVERYTHING IS ALREADY THE WAY IT'S GOING TO BE
IT'S ALWAYS GOING TO STAY THAT WAY DON'T THEY SEE?

I'M NOT GOING TO PRETEND OR HESITATE ANY LONGER
EVERYONE IS GOING TO SEE THE REAL ME THE WAY I'VE BEEN

THERE'S NO MORE PRETENDING IN MY LIFE NOT FOR ANYONE
I'M NOT GOING TO PRETEND THAT EVERYTHING IS FINE

I'M NOT GOING TO PRETEND THAT I'M NOT HURTING INSIDE
THAT I'VE BEEN HURTING SINCE I WAS A LITTLE BABY GIRL

I WANT EVERYONE TO SEE THAT ONLY YOU HAD MY HEART
BUT THE ANGELS FROM HEAVEN CAME THEY TOOK YOU AWAY

I KNEW THAT HE WASN'T GOING TO LET MY HAPPINESS STAY
I ALSO KNEW IN MY HEART YOU WOULDN'T BE HERE FOR LONG

SO THERE'S NO MORE PRETENDING THAT I'M HAPPY HERE AT ALL
FOR I'M NOT HAPPY I'M SAD I'M HURT AND I WANT TO GO HOME

I MISS YOU I MISS THE ONLY ONE THAT EVER LOVED ME FOR
REALS
I HURT INSIDE FOR THERE'S ONLY TEARS NOW THAT YOU'RE
GONE

ROSE PORTILLO

Saved

She's been criticized and judged
Her spirit has been stomped in mud
Inside she suffers and cries
It takes someone different
To really understand why

She walks around and smiles
But all alone she weeps
Out of insecurity she needs to climb
At night she cries herself to sleep
Not knowing if she'll wake up in the morning

Emptiness are her thoughts
Memories are of her family
Who have done nothing but fought
It's so hard being a teen especially
One who has seen what she has seen

She's been called a loser and a geek
On good days she's often been called a freak
She's over stressed and way underweight
Her straight black hair covers her face
Only her smile has faded away

Along with her personality every passing day
She prefers not to speak though her voice is weak
On some nights she stays so awake
Looking at the scars on her wrists
That she knows will not fade away

Her grades are low as is her self esteem
She never knew the devil could be so mean
She glances at a bible not ever having known
What it means or reads about inside
She has a heart that has been so torn

Four years later she's beautiful and bright
Feeling this because her eyes were opened to light
In the Grace of God and in a Rainbow of Happiness
You can see her just singing and dancing
She is smiling ear to ear for she has been Saved!

Nessie

My Dearest Peanut

My Dearest Peanut, My Love, So Long Ago Still I Love
As I Remember You Were In My Arms So Loving, So Bold
Why Did You Do What You Did For All I Wanted Was You
Why Would You Want To Leave Me I Was Coming Home!

I'm Sorry That I Was Such A Disappointment For You
Please Forgive Me If I Hurt You, I Really Didn't Mean To
I Think Of Those Nights Me And You, Oh I Miss You So
I Dream I Wish You Were Lying Here With Me Once More

I Cry Every Day, Tears Of Love, Nights Of Such Loneliness!
You Are The One I Love The Only One I Always Dream Of
It's Not Fair To Anyone Who Say They Love Me, I Suppose
They Could Never Compare To You Or The Love You Showed

"My Love," You Are So Instilled In My Life, Where Did You Go?
How Do I Live? How Do I Go On Without You? You Are My Soul
Waiting For You To Come Into My Dreams, For You To Come Home!
Every Dark Night In The Cold Waiting To See You My Endless Woes

Knowing That You Can Never Come Back For They Buried You!
Why Didn't They Leave Us Alone? I Thought It Was A Bad Joke
Please Dear Lord Please Bring My Baby, Bring Him Back Home!
I Am All Alone, I Can't Survive Without You, Yes I Miss You So!

Where Did You Go? To What Realm Do You Roam? Take Me Too!
Where Does Your Spirit Fly? Do You Come To See Me? Do I Know?
Where Does Your Spirit Lie? You're Just Buried In The Ground
I Can't See You, I Can't Find You, I'm Searching For Your Soul!

Minu

Awful Pain

So many damn pills I drink for this awful pain
Yet nothing do they do for the pain is so deep so strong
Praying each time I take them that they just take it away
Only in vain now everything in my life seems to be drugs

I have never taken drugs in my life though I did judge
I let go of "The Love of My Life" all because of his drugs
Thinking I was doing the right thing for him and me
Now this great awful pain in my body reminds of his pain

What can I do with this forsaken horrible illness today
It stays inside my veins as punishment it won't go away
Even as I sleep I feel pain with every morning as I awake
As I open my eyes I feel this awful pain I will never rest

I don't want to live anymore for the pain just won't leave
As the tears run down my face praying and crying for relief
Wishing sometimes that someone somewhere can help me
Moaning all the while tossing turning without understanding

No one can hold me for their touch burns twice as much!
Crying for all eternity looking for him I cannot even be hugged
Maybe somehow this awful pain of mine seems to remind me
Of the all great judgments I put on The Love of My Life's life

Rose Portillo

Si Tu Conociste A Mi Madrina

Si Tu Conociste A Mi Madrina, Tu Supieras
Ella Era Una Mujer Muy Buena Y Cariniosa
Con Un Corazon Mas Precioso De Plata De Oro
Con Juicio Y Bondad, Que Nunca A Contado

Benditos Son Los Que Conocieron Su Amor
Porque Si Tu Conociste A Mi Madrina, Tu Supieras
Ella Era Una Mujer Hermosa, Tan Dado De Su Alma
En Verdad, Ella Tiene Una Parte Especial En El Cielo, Con Dios

Si Tu Conociste A Mi Madrina, Tu Supieras
Que Ella Ya Va Entrando Las Puertas Sagrados Del Cielo
Yo Voy A Sonrir Y Sentir Su Amor Cuando Miro Las Estrellas
Supiendo Que Por El Resto De Eternidad Estara En Los Brazos De Dios

Seguramente, Ella Es Una Paloma Divina De Dios
Que Ahora Sera Abrasada Eternamente En El Gran Amor
Por Favor, Digale Que Me Perdone, Dios Santo
Por No Ensenar Que Era Especial Y En Verdad Es, Y Siempre Lo Sera

Si Tu Conociste A Mi Madrina, Tu Supieras
Que No Falta Un Angel En El Cielo, No Mas
La Encontraron Y La Llevaran A Honde Ella Perteneste
Por Nuestro Padre, El Mismo, Vino A Llevar La A Su Casa

If You Knew My God Mother

If You Knew My God Mother, You'd Know
She Was Such A Good Person And So Lovable
With A Heart So Precious Like A Plate Of Gold
A Bond Of Loyalty Not Many Had Or Could Compare

Whoever Knew My God Mother You Were Blessed
Because If You Knew My God Mother, You'd Know
She Was Very Beautiful Always Inside Within Her Soul
In Truth, She Has A Special Place In Heaven With God

If You Knew My God Mother, You'd Know
She Will Pass Right Through The Doors Of Heaven
I Will Smile As I Think Of Her Love And Look At The Stars
For The Rest Of Eternity She Will Be In The Arms Of God

Surely, She Is A Divine Dove From The Heavens Of The Lord
I Know She Will Be Embraced Eternally With His Grand Love
Please, God, Please Ask Her To Forgive Me Though
For Not Showing How Special She Was And She Will Always Be

If You Knew My God Mother, You'd Know
That There Is One Of Their Angels No Longer Left Here
They Have Taken Her From This Earth To Where She Belongs
For God Knew All Along Her Beautiful Heart And Soul

Minu Portillo

Lilly & Felice;
(Jaguar & Aimee)

Why you were playing in this garden
Staying inside why were you so afraid?

Fear of the deep secret finally being revealed
All of them playing all their death filled games

For the love of your heart though she is so dear
Living only to hold her to always keep her near

Before her friends your enemies take you away
Hoping praying they will never find out today

Lovers at the sight of eachother so beautiful
Both victims of each other's world waiting to end

If you're ever caught it would surely mean death
You were each other's lovers all of each other's lives

******

Now caught we were as your people took me away
Where will you be "My Love" of where can I see?

Will I ever see you again look into your loving eyes?
Will you ever find me sorry but I needed you to go

A love that lasts forever she always did say
A love that even forever couldn't bear her tears

I too feel the pain of a love forever like you two
For me too my Forever Love was gone too soon

Rose Portillo

I'm Not Trying

You know I've tried so hard to forget I did forget
But how? It's so hard to forget the other part of me

Knowing that I'm not the same without it
Knowing I don't want to exist without it any longer

Knowing that I don't even want to be around
I wake up wondering why is it I'm still here

I've been with someone and yes it helps
But when lately all I've been doing is nothing

Is crying because I can't find you again I'm trying
All he's been doing is not helping me forget

All he's been doing is bringing you home back to me
When he makes me cry he brings to me your memory

Home back to me back in my mind inside my brain
I'm not trying to forget any longer I will go insane

Rose Portillo

Since You've Been Gone

Since you've been gone all I've have felt is alone
I've done nothing but cry some lonely nights long

Since you've been gone my tears never seem to end
As I look around I remember "My Angel" is gone

Since you've been gone I still don't understand why
Why you had to leave because you said you'd never go

Since you've been gone no one's around no one's my hero
There's no more "Me and You" this ugly pain cutting so deep

Since you've been gone I see no future as I search for you
I can't seem to find you it hurts I feel it's over and so done

You left me with such a huge hole that I simply cannot fill
Since you've been gone tomorrow seems so sad I still alone

You were the only thing that mattered in this whole world
Since you've been gone nothing seems worth living for

I tried to ask "The Boss" if with you at least I could go
Since you've been gone that's all I ever want to do now

Remember when you and I would lay together "alone"
Since you've been gone I don't even want to live anymore

Because since you've been gone "My Love of Mine"
My life is over seeming to have no meaning any longer

Rose Portillo

The Day You Left My World

The Day You Left My World So Tortured I Was In My Mind,
Wait, My Heart Stopped My World Ended, Where Were You?
I Blocked Out Everyone And What The Hell They All Said,
They Said Sorry I Couldn't Hear Them Why? You Were Gone.

I Waited For You To Come Show Them They Were Wrong,
All Those Mean Rotten People, They Said You Were Dead!
I Waited For You To Come Back, To Quietly Bring Me Home,
To Save Me From This Wretched, Condemned, Ugly World!

I Waited That Night Feeling Like Running Somewhere, Anywhere,
Suffocated, Choked And Believing It Was Just One Of Your Jokes!
Hearing The Lies, I Couldn't Move I Just Sat There, I Was Dead,
You Weren't Dead, For You Would Have Kissed Me In Return.

The Day You Left My World, It Was I That Invokingly Truly Died,
It Was Somewhere Inside Of All The Hatred And All My Lies.
I Worried, I Still Worry, Where You Had To Go, Can I Go Too?
Why Didn't I Go? Your Death Was All That I Had Ever Dread.

The Day You Left My World, I Was Scared For You, Why You?
It Wasn't Fair For You To Be So All Alone, Life Is So Cruel Alone.
The Guilt I Bore Forever Still For Leaving, Was On Me Not You,
I Was Coming Back, But I Know You Thought I Left You For Good.

I Wish I Could Take It All Back, To Turn The Great Big Clock,
I Wish I Could Change The Hands Of Time, To Send Time Behind.
To Prevent The Hurt I Caused You And Again Make You Mine,
The Day You Left My World, My Eyes, My Heart Went So Blind.

I Really Left My Mind, I Couldn't Hear, Holding All Within To Hide,
I Didn't Want To See, I Wouldn't Speak To Anyone, For What?
Why Should I Be Alive? More Importantly, Why Should I Be Happy?
There Was No More Time, All Time Left Too, When You Died.

Deafening Stillness, My Thick Mental Illness, Now Set In For Good!
Never Smiling Again, For What? My Smiles Were Gone With You!
It Hurt Me, Who Cares Now, You Left I Didn't Deserve It, No How,
I Wanted No One, Nothing, Only You, And Never You Did I Find.

The Day You Left My World, I Became No One's Girl Not Even Mine,
The Melancholic, So Sad, Too Bad, Not Enough, Until This Very Day.
There Isn't Anything Or Anyone Can Do Or Anyone Can Ever Say, Nothing,
The Girl You Knew Is Gone, She Died Too, The Day You Left My World.

Rose Portillo

My Brown Eyes Blue

SINCE YOU LEFT I JUST WANT YOU TO KNOW
I WAIT AND WAIT I DON'T KNOW WHY BUT I DO

NO ONE ELSE IS HERE NO MATTER WHAT I TRY
NO MATTER WHERE I LOOK NOW I'M TIRED TOO

THE SECRETS WERE JUST FOR FUN YOU KNEW THAT
ONLY TO SHOW HOW MUCH I REALLY LOVE YOU

I NEVER THOUGHT THAT YOU WOULD EVER LEAVE ME
I'M SO BLUE I DIDN'T MEAN TO TREAT YOU SO MEAN

I KNEW I'D CRY I'VE NEVER BEEN SO BLUE IN MY LIFE
EXCEPT EVERY TIME I'D LIE NEXT TO YOU I KNEW

FOR I FELT THE FUTURE OF YOU NOT BEING NEAR ME
NOT BEING WITH ME TO THE END AND YOU BEING GONE

SINCE YOU LEFT ME IN THIS UGLY WORLD I'VE BEEN BLUE
I TOLD YOU THEY WOULD HURT ME I KNEW IT WAS TRUE

YOU DIDN'T WANT TO HURT ME THIS WAS AS YOU EXISTED
BUT YOU WENT AWAY YOU HURT ME YOU DID IT ANYWAY

SINCE YOU LEFT ME YES MY BROWN EYES ARE SO BLUE
THERE'S NO ONE HERE BABY I DON'T KNOW WHAT TO DO

ROSE PORTILLO

Our Souls Reaching Heaven

IT SEEMED AT FIRST WHEN YOU LEFT THIS WORLD
IT WAS FOR NO REASON THAT SEEMED TO BE FIT

AS I LOOK BACK AT IT IN A DIFFERENT VIEW NOW
THERE IS A REASON FOR WHAT HAPPENED UNFURLED

WAS IT BECAUSE FOR ME YOUR SOUL HAD ALWAYS BEEN
IS IT BECAUSE OUR TIME TOGETHER REALLY HAS NO END

TIME IS ON OUR SIDE FOR YEARS ARE MERE SECONDS
CAN ONE WHO JUST VANISHED IN A MINUTE LAST FOREVER

YET WHAT SEEMS FOREVER IS FOR MERELY ONLY A MINUTE
THEN MAYBE WHAT LIES BETWEEN US CAN NEVER BE GONE

IS THAT WE KEEP CROSSING BEYOND DIMENSIONS WE ARE IN
ONLY TO FIND IT IS WHERE OUR FATE IS TO BEGIN AGAIN

YOU HAVE NEVER LEFT ME AS I ONCE ALWAYS FEARED
AS I CRIED SO ANGRY THAT YOU LEFT ME ALONE HERE

SINCE YOUR SOUL'S ALWAYS INTRIGUINGLY STILL WITH MINE
HAVING BECOME MY VERY ESSENCE SINCE OUR LOVE'S DAWN

ONLY TO RETURN TO YOUR ESSENCE FOREVER BEING TIED
FOR WITH YOU THERE IS NO DENYING OF OUR ENDLESS LIVES

INSIDE OUR CIRCLE OF TIME THE ERRS THERE IS NO TRYING
FOR WE ARE STILL LYING ENTWINED TOGETHER FOR ALL TIME

TO BECOME WHAT WE HAVE ALWAYS BEEN FOREVER SAVING
EACHOTHER'S LOVES OUR HEARTS EACH EON WE'RE STAYING IN

SO FEAR I SHOULD NOT FOR ME IT IS YOUR SPIRIT STILL AWAITS
NOT FOR LONG AGAIN FOR YOU FOR ME ARE STILL OUR ONLY
FATES

DESTINY OUR LIVE'S LOVE ALWAYS SEARCHING FULFILLING
WITHIN
TRYING OVER AND OVER AGAIN TIL OUR SOULS REACHING
HEAVEN

ROSE PORTILLO

Our Tainted Love

So Many Hateful Ugly People Trying To End Our Love
Their Plots Hurting Our Love Tainting It So Much Still
Why Can't They Leave Us Alone Why Do They Hate Us
A True Love Why Do They Pry In Our Lives It's Enough

From The Beginning To Even Now Their Hatred Grows
You Can Hear All Their Hateful Thoughts All Their Lies
They Never Wanted Us To Have The Love That We Feel
They Want Us With No One Except For Whom They Say

There Is A Strong Evil That Still Exists In My World
Evil Spirits That Hate Me And All Whom I Love Inside
Though Our Love So Strong Damaged Hearts Was Done
Separating Us From Each Other Causing Hurt Forever

Years Alone Yearning To Hold My Loved One So Dear
Tired Of Allowing Hatred To Stay Between Our Hearts
Sorry Now For All The Years Without Him Without Me
Still In Love Though We Found No Matter What Was To Be

Anxious And Hurt We Searched For Our Love To Find Again
When He Knew Of Me Near Him So Loving So Afraid Of Them
So Still In Love With Each Other We Knew Nothing More
Forgetting Their Lies Accepting Our Love Forgiving Our Sins

All That Was Done Forever We Wanted To Erase To Just Love
In The Heap Of Our Anxious Hearts Joined Together From Then
We Loved So Dear So Much The Universe Could Hear Us Again
Forever Again Was Our Vow To Never Die Without One Another

Suddenly It Changed The Course We Took Finally We Arrived
It Drove Us To Do Our Plan In Different Temporary Paths
Only To Unite With Each Other For All Of Our Permanent Lives
Yes It Happened As He Chose One False Move On His Part

He Turned Looked The Other Way One Second Without Me There
He Stopped He Listened To Their Hatred Their Lies He Heard
He Succombed To Their Wishes This Time Now It Was His Sin
He Left Me He Left My World Their Hatred Him They Did Kill

Minu Portillo

Never Goodbye

What Does One Do As Gone Is Anew
When One Held A Promise Ever So True
A Promise That One Has Held Onto As Life
With All Their Heart And All Their Might

Where Does That Promise Held On To Go?
What Happens To Vows Having Been Given?
Ringing Out To The Universe We Live With
For All Life As One Witnessed To Ever Float

Does The Promise Forever More Get Lost?
Among The Universe Where Ever One Dies
Does The Promise Hold Dear For No Matter
With Spirits Having Promised Stuck In Afterlife?

A Promise So Binding For A One Love So Fierce
Oh So Strong But Does Love's Promise Hold On
Tightly Filled With Strong Love Burning Through
Do They Feel Each Soul's Entwined Deep Within

As Ever Someone Will Hold On To A Promise
You Cling To The Love Once Given In The Night
Your Whole Soul Lives On Depending Upon This
Forever With All Your Life And All Your Might

What Does One Do With The Promise So True
Does The Promise Linger Waiting To Be Done
Or Will The Promise Just Sit Idle In The Universe?
A Loved One Who Left The Promise Has Died

Where Does His Promise Go? Now What Do I Do?
To Hold Onto The Promise You've Given To Me
Promise Of Your Love Is To Me A Never Goodbye
To Stay Forever Always Loving Me Even In Afterlife

When Will The Promise You Gave To Me Come True
If Your Life Here Is Done For Now Is All Through?
Where Can I Find You I Ask Is The Question For You
Where Do I Find Your Promise You Left Me So Blue

Did My Loved One Take It With Him And His Souls
As His Spirit Gone Somewhere In The Universe I Wait
Will I Ever Find This Beautiful Vow He Made To Me
He Promised To Love Me Forever For All Eternity

A Promise That He Vowed Never To Leave Me Alone
A Promise He Made To Me With All Heart And Soul
Tell Me Someone Please Tell Forever What Can I Do?
Now What Do I Do? For I Still Sit I Still Wait Forever

I Will Always Hold On To This Promise As I Live
Made With Love So Sincere So Dearly He Gives
Though Left Here Alone With My Heart So Broken
Sitting In Tears With His And My Never Goodbye

I Sang To His Soul The Words Of All Love Songs
Never Ever Stop Loving Him My Love To Be Forever
He Gave Me His Very Word To Stay With Me True
He Vowed He'd Never Leave Me Alone So Cruel

I Wait With All My Hurt Heart Moaning I Still Cry
All Of The Universe Aloud For All The Stars To Hear
Please Come Back Home To Me Tell Me It's A Lie
Please Keep Your Promise Made With Love So True

Minu Portillo